To my Journalist
Herman Roe
with my Compliments
[illegible] Miller
August 8-1958

A. Q. Miller, Sr., interpreter of the Kansas scene for over sixty years; publisher of the BELLEVILLE TELESCOPE, *one of the nation's outstanding weeklies, and one of Kansas most loyal sons.*

A Biography of A. Q. Miller, Sr.

JAYHAWK EDITOR

COMPILED AND EDITED BY

James D. Callahan

FROM THE RECOLLECTIONS, WRITINGS AND PAPERS OF

A. Q. Miller, Sr.

PUBLISHED BY
STERLING PRESS
LOS ANGELES, CALIFORNIA, U.S.A.

FIRST EDITION

For Martha Patterson Miller

Because it is the story of my life, I have been asked to dedicate this book. I am grateful for the opportunity.

Without the love, understanding and encouragement of my wife there, very possibly, wouldn't be anything to write a book about.

While I am proud of my career as a country editor and the contributions toward the welfare of my community and state that this career made possible, I am infinitely more proud of my fine "journalistic" family.

To Martha Patterson Miller must go the credit for rearing these fine children, patiently and understandingly in a Christian atmosphere. Today their lives and careers reflect the principles of honesty and integrity they learned from their mother.

As our sixtieth wedding anniversary nears, I can look back on a full and happy life and, I feel, a useful one because of Martha Patterson Miller to whom I dedicate this book and to whom I am forever dedicated.

A. Q. MILLER, SR.

CONTENTS

List of Illustrations

CHAPTER I

CHAPTER I

The Turbulent Kansas Scene

HERITAGE OF A. Q. MILLER, SR.

IN NO OTHER COUNTRY of the world has the newspaper played such an important role in the life of a nation as it has in the United States of America. Of all newspaper categories, the greatest debt is probably owed to the weekly, the country weekly. During the nation's formative years there was no other means of communicating information to its citizens, it was left to the country editor to print the news as he gathered it and then interpret that news by means of editorials. Opinions were formed and votes were cast on the basis of information contained in the country weekly—in many areas they still are.

Kansas has been privileged to have what is generally acknowledged as the most eloquent press in the United States. Fame has come to the Kansas press, not because of a few great metropolitan newspapers, but because of the consistent hard hitting journalism of its many virile weekly newspapers and the integrity of the men who edit these publications.

To understand the Kansas press one must know something about the heritage of Kansas. At the conclusion of the bloody Civil War, Kansas was hailed as the land of opportunity. In

1865 veterans of the strife were welcomed home to Leavenworth by a grand peace jubilee. Torn battle flags with the historic names of Gettysburg, Antietam, Shiloh and the Wilderness were cased forever.

The nation's railroads were pushing west, following the tracks of Indian dog sleds, covered wagons, the pony express and the stage coach. Along the railroad right of ways, telegraph poles marked extension of verbal communication.

In 1863 the railroad entered Kansas at Wyandotte. By the next year it had reached Lawrence and in 1865, despite the war, the railroad was at Topeka. In 1870 the iron trail had traversed the prairies to Denver. Federal land grants made the railroad's passage through Kansas possible. Ten million acres in strips twenty miles wide were made available to the Kansas Pacific (now Union Pacific) and another ten million acres were given to the Santa Fe.

To push the railroad through Kansas thousands of laborers were necessary. Most of these were veterans of the Civil War recently discharged from the service. Needless to say, the terrific influx of transient population created problems for the new territory. Towns which sprang up along the right of ways were wide open, vice was rampant. Mingled with the hardy railroad construction workers were cattlemen who had driven their herds to the new rail heads. These cowhands were tired and thirsty and looking for relaxation by the time they had consigned their charges to the railroad. The two strata of frontier society, the railroaders and the cattlemen, often clashed violently.

The law in Kansas, at this time, was the best fist fighter or the fastest man on the draw with a Colt or a Winchester. Arguments were settled quickly by these means. Dodge City's "Boot Hill" cemetery is typical of the resting places that awaited those who lost an argument. Such law and order as there was soon came to be symbolized by rugged frontier marshals like "Bat" Masterson, "Wild Bill" Hickok and Wyatt Earp.

About this time a young professional buffalo hunter became known for his prowess with a rifle. William F. Cody had a contract to supply fresh buffalo meat to the Kansas Pacific workers. Partly by honest achievement, partly by high powered press agentry, Cody soon became known to a new generation as "Buffalo Bill," hero of the wild west.

Indians along the Kansas prairie deeply resented the westward push of civilization. Their hunting grounds were being lost to the white man on an increasing scale. Ignoring peace treaties, the desperate Indians harassed track laying crews continually. Putting an end to the Indian raids brought further fame to two war hardened cavalrymen: Phil Sheridan and George Armstrong Custer.

In 1873 settlers taking advantage of the federal homestead laws had filed for 26 million acres of Kansas land. To fulfill homestead requirements the government required five consecutive years of occupancy. Veterans were given occupancy credit for their time in the army. Kansas population soon reached almost 400,000. It seemed that the fledgling state had a bright future and would soon outgrow its colorful early history. But the future was to present further problems.

A nation-wide financial panic hit the Middle West hard and just as Kansas farmers were getting their second wind, a relentless drought devastated the plains. Along with the drought came an eerie, terrifying invasion.

On a bright July morning in 1874, when A. Q. Miller, Sr., was five months old, farmers all over Kansas were anxiously watching the skies. There hadn't been a drop of rain for months. On the horizon they saw a cloud. It rose in the northwest and filled the sky. As it grew closer the farmers could see that the sun reflected from the bodies of millions of grasshoppers.

Wherever the cloud settled on the land the area was devastated; new grass and summer foliage vanished in just a few minutes. There was no grain that summer — no corn, feed, or grass. Cattle starved all over the state. The grasshopper plague caused trains to slither to a stop on swarms of the greasy bodied insects; wells and springs were clogged with dead grasshoppers. They were everywhere. The presence of the grasshoppers continued until cold weather set in. They disappeared, returning only briefly the next year and have never been heard from since. The indomitable Kansans survived this terrifying blight although for many years their dreams were haunted with swarms of grasshoppers.

Kansas began to make cultural strides from its earliest pioneer days. Baker University was founded at Baldwin in 1858; the Kansas State College of Agriculture and Applied Science at Manhattan in 1863 and State Normal (Teachers') at Emporia in 1865. In 1866 the buildings of the University of Kansas at Lawrence started to rise.

Prohibition, later to be conducted unsuccessfully on a national scale, appeared early on the Kansas scene. There is no doubt that Kansas sentiment in regard to prohibition was prompted by the frontier excesses that marked the growth of the territory. As the transients began to be replaced by permanent citizens with families to rear, attempts were made to put a damper on the "wild west."

A clause in the territorial Wyandotte constitution, defeated by 31 to 19, had prohibited the saloon. But it was not allowed to die. In 1880 a constitutional amendment was adopted banning liquor and the saloon. Enforcement of this law was difficult. Local authorities were unenthusiastic and violations were punished by token fines. Late in the 1880's, a plump, motherly woman in her forties began a one woman crusade against liquor that was to attract national attention. Carrie Nation was shocked and disappointed at the antipathy of the public toward Kansas prohibition laws. Carrie's crusade, characterized at first by saloon smashing with rocks and later with the famous hatchet, spread all over the United States and had counterparts in the British Isles. Carrie died in 1911 before her dream of national prohibition could be realized. Carrie Nation was one of a long line of Kansas' "rugged individualists" who were to make their presence known to the nation.

About the time that Carrie Nation was engaged in her saloon smashing career, another campaign had started in Kansas that was to have national repercussions, the Populist movement. Populism had its roots in the days immediately following the Civil War. The growth of mechanization in industry had created a large scale unemployment problem. A few men, capitalizing on the inventive genius of the nation, had, by virtue of their enterprise, concentrated a large part of the nation's wealth in their hands. Many of these men failed to realize the responsibilities accompanying such great power. As this concentration of wealth occurred, a new social consciousness began to arise. A large number of writers, including essayists and novelists, began striking blows against exploitation of the poor. These literary personalities included such men as Walt Whitman, John Ruskin, George Bernard Shaw and Charles Dickens.

As far as the volume of socially conscious literature is concerned, it is doubtful if very many Kansans were affected by it. They were too busy working to do much extensive reading. But Kansans felt very keenly about the dignity of labor. It was one of the first states to pay heed to the changing political ideology resulting from social unrest. This change reached a climax in the last decade of the nineteenth century.

What actually took place was a bloodless revolution. Kansas had been Republican from the time the party was founded. In 1888 Kansas stood at the head of the nation as far as fidelity to the Republican party was concerned. It returned a greater majority for Republican candidate Benjamin Harrison than did any other state.

But Kansas' sentiment was changing. The Farmers' Alliance, an organization dedicated to aiding its members politically and financially, which was organized in Texas, spread to Kansas. By 1890 it had over 100,000 members in Kansas. This Kansas membership became the nucleus of the Populist Party, the first major group in the nation to break away from the two traditional and great political parties. Known at first as the People's Party, it attracted voters who resented the extravagances of the newly rich and the private monopoly which existed in public commodities. The Populist Party kept the country in an uproar for almost a quarter of a century.

The ideal responsible for the Populist Party was as old as civilization but the way it was handled was unique. William E. Connelley, distinguished historian, aptly characterizes the movement: "It was not Populism that distinguished Kansas but Kansas that distinguished Populism."

Born a few months before the start of the "grasshopper blight" during Kansas' blustering frontier era, A. Q. Miller, Sr., grew up to set type and write his fledgling editorials at the height of the colorful Populist movement.

While Kansas, like other states, has had its scandals and its political misfits, no administration or individual officer has long been able to operate to the detriment of the state. The watchdogs of the sovereign state of Kansas were ever vigilant. Once determined that any individual, or group of individuals, sought personal aggrandizement or enrichment before the welfare of his state, the Kansas weeklies went to work on him. Spotlighted by the fearless editorials and factual news stories of the zealous weeklies, the individual involved generally resigned before being driven from public office in the next election.

Kansas has many fine weekly newspapers and many sterling editors. The Kansas editor is a unique brand of journalist. He is proud of his state and proud of his profession. Such fame as has come to him he considers incidental to his real mission — doing the very best he can for his community and the state of Kansas.

Kansas editors are not hesitant about taking a stand on an issue. Once convinced that the course they have set for themselves is the right one, they pull no punches. The result has been some of the finest journalism to be found in America today.

Belleville, Kansas, is the county seat of Republic County. It is the home of *The Belleville Telescope,* established in 1870. This dynamic weekly newspaper has been published by A. Q. Miller, Sr., for over fifty years. In a county with a total population of more than 15,000, the Telescope circulates over 4,000 copies. This means it goes into practically every home in Republic County.

A. Q. Miller, Sr., is considered one of Kansas' outstanding journalists, and with the quality of Kansas journalism what it is, this is no insignificant honor. His story and the story of his paper is an interesting one. Born and reared in Kansas, A. Q. Miller has contributed much to the welfare of his state and his country. These contributions were made possible by his journalistic efforts, his vision and foresight, and his courage in championing those things he believed right and denouncing those things he believed wrong. His story is a tribute to himself and the hundreds of other editors of the nation's country weeklies who have devoted their lives to their communities.

Perhaps no greater tribute can be paid any man than to say that he lived a full and useful life. This can be said of A. Q. Miller who as a newspaperman did so much for his community and his state; as a citizen took such a full and active part in the activities of his community, serving wherever he could; and as a husband and father reared a family that is continuing the tradition of professional and civic usefulness because of the example that he and his wife, Martha, set for them.

Much has been written concerning heredity and the part that it plays in the formation of an individual's character. It is not the purpose of this book to argue the premise pro or con. In the case of A. Q. Miller, Sr., it would seem that his inherent honesty, devotion to duty, and desire to serve his fellow man, are traits that he acquired from his parents. It is certain that his own children absorbed these attributes from A. Q. and his beloved wife, Martha.

His father, J. T. Miller, was born in Benton County, Iowa, in 1845. His typically American ancestry comprised forebears of German, Irish and Scotch. When only seventeen years old, he volunteered for service in the Federal army and participated in the historic battle of Shiloh, Tennessee. Here he was taken prisoner by the Confederates in 1862. Prior to being captured his health had already been seriously impaired by a severe attack of measles. Facilities in the prison camp were inadequate and his already weakened condition grew worse. At first opportunity he was exchanged by the Confederate Army and shortly thereafter invalided out of the service.

Manifesting what appears to be a lasting Miller trait, unwillingness to accept something for nothing, J. T. Miller steadfastly refused to request a Federal pension of eight dollars a month to which his damaged health entitled him. The determined young veteran did not feel he was yet ready to become a ward of the government. In the last years of his life, when totally incapacitated, J. T. Miller put in for his small pension.

Immediately following the Civil War, the elder Miller became a country school teacher in Benton County. America's educational system of that day was a far cry from the modern, streamlined operation of the twentieth century. Still in his teens,

A. Q. Miller's parents: J. T. Miller and *Marie Cantonwine Miller, who settled on a rugged Kansas homestead near Peat's Creek immediately after the Civil War.*

the young schoolmaster found that he had to stay up nights studying in order to keep ahead of his class.

J. T. Miller married Marie Cantonwine at Vinton, Iowa, in 1869. The Homestead Act, giving free lands to Union soldiers, had been passed and the newly married Millers discussed taking up a homestead in the young state of Kansas. A move of this nature was not one to be lightly made. This was a new country, strange and even primitive. Certainly, while the opportunities would be greater, the hazards would be commensurate. Weighing all the factors, the Millers acted. They took up a homestead on a rugged piece of land by Peat's Creek, south of the frontier town of Palmer, Kansas.

CHAPTER II

Early Years In Journalism

FROM PRINTER'S DEVIL TO EDITOR

ALEXANDER QUINTELLA MILLER was born in a thatched roof hut, situated on a rocky Kansas homestead, on February 7, 1874. His childhood was a normal one. His parents provided for their family to the best of their ability. While there was no poverty, neither was there always plenty. His father was engaged in the mercantile business. Income from the small general store at Peat's Creek was supplemented by the crops grown on the homestead.

As the family grew, A. Q. had three sisters, the elder Miller expanded his mercantile business, the main store finally being located in Clifton. The word "finally" is used because in this era of railroad expansion it took a shrewd businessman to guess where the "right of ways" were going and locate along one of them. The business was shifted several times before being permanently located in Clifton.

The route of the railroads pushing continually westward for many years determined the fate and prosperity of townships. Where the "right of way" went through there was an immediate business boom. Many of the by-passed towns became "ghost towns." J. T. Miller located correctly when he moved the business "finally" to Clifton and his enterprise prospered.

A. Q., or Quin as he preferred to be known, attended the Clifton schools and helped around his father's store. The country store was the nineteenth century counterpart of the present day radio or television newscast. News and views on all subjects, especially politics, were exchanged and evaluated around the pot bellied stove in the winter and the porch benches in the summer. Perhaps it was this apprenticeship in the store, where young Quin took up an unobtrusive position within hearing distance of his elders, that helped develop Miller's keen interest in political affairs.

With high school graduation approaching, Miller decided that he did not care for country store keeping as a vocation. Farming, he reasoned, offered much greater opportunities. Young men of middle class families in that day did not attend college. In fact, very few of them graduated from high school.

Immediately upon graduating, Quin Miller sought employment on the farm of a neighbor, John Cooper. He operated a cultivator drawn by a team of mules. Small of stature, he had to climb up on a manger to bridle the mules. When he finally succeeded in bridling them, Quin started across the fields like a man possessed. Having no idea of the amount of work expected from a new farm hand, the conscientious apprentice drove himself frantically from dawn to dusk, sparing neither himself nor the mules.

After the one summer on the farm, Quin's parents decided that he just wasn't cut out for the agricultural life. Picking the straw out of his hair and outfitting him in new clothes — he had outgrown his others — they dispatched him to the local barber shop to be shorn of several weeks' growth of hair.

From Quin's point of view the summer was not wasted. While working on the Cooper farm he got his first glimpse of the girl who was to become his wife. The young farmhand, sad to say, did not greatly impress the young lady at the time.

A sister of Martha Patterson, the future Mrs. Miller, asked her who was the bedraggled lad riding by the Patterson place on a spotted pony. "Just some town boy working for John Cooper, I suppose," was Martha's laconic reply.

Quin Miller and Martha Patterson were born and reared only ten miles apart, yet they had never met. A few years after the encounter mentioned above, the Pattersons moved to Clifton because of the better educational opportunities it afforded the girls. Quin met Martha, formally, at a party when he made a backward move and inadvertently stepped on her foot. To this day he will not divulge if it was planned strategy or accident. From the time of the "toe stepping" the friendship flowered.

Shortly after his farming interlude, Quin Miller heard that the *Clifton News* was looking for a printer's devil. Although he hadn't the vaguest idea of what this entailed, Quin applied for and got the job.

From the day he first donned his apron in the shop of the *Clifton News,* A. Q. Miller, Sr., has never been long away from the smell of printer's ink or the clicking of typewriters. Although not realizing it at this time, he had found the work that was to make his life a useful and beneficial one.

A. Q. Miller's recollections of his first years as a newspaperman, which began when he was seventeen years old, are best told in his own characteristic manner:

"When I first went to work for the *Clifton News,* I hadn't the vaguest idea what a printer's devil did. I soon found out. My first assigned task was to mail the single wrappers, individual copies of the newspaper. Flour paste was mixed and used to seal the wrappers. I can still vividly recall the odor exuding from the unused paste after the job was completed. The shop took on all the fragrance of a packing plant.

"In this day all type in country newspaper offices was hand set. I liked using the composing stick and it wasn't long until I could set a stick of long primer type, leaded, in fourteen minutes. Now this probably doesn't sound like any great feat, but in the 1890's it was.

"Office equipment was crude. The only power available was hand power and I was called upon to furnish most of that. We had a Prouty flat bed news press with a handle bolted to the fly wheel. The paper was hand folded on a long table. Quarto paper with four pages of Western Newspaper Union ready print was cut with twine string for mailing. The shop also contained a nine by twelve Gordon job press operated by a foot lever. On the Gordon I could kick off 500 envelopes, a $1.75 order, in twenty minutes. This was the extent of our equipment in the shop. The news and the display room boasted a counter and a couple of badly battered desks. There were several fonts of news and display type. Two much used items, a broom and the lone community office towel, were secluded behind the front door.

"Clifton, a town with a population of 450 people, contained two weekly newspapers. In 1892 a third newspaper came to town. With much fanfare it announced that it was operating a steam printing plant. The steam printing plant was a revolutionary innovation at that time and I was beside myself with curiosity to see this printing behemoth. Finally I got an opportunity to view our modern well-equipped rival. I hurried down the street, prepared to be awed. The 'steam printing plant' was a fifteen by twenty-four inch job press which printed the newspaper and such job printing as came into the shop, one page at a time. Attached to the flywheel of the press by a leather belt was a one cylinder gasoline engine—the 'steam' phase of the operation. Although I had to admit that the motor, had it functioned as it should, would have been a great improvement over the 'Miller' power which operated most of the *Clifton News* equipment, the third newspaper's printing facilities were quite a letdown.

"During the several years I worked on the *Clifton News* there were three different managements. I went along with the shop inventory as each transfer took place. I had little concern with the higher echelons of publishing as long as my weekly salary was forthcoming.

"Top wages for a country printer at this time were $5.00 a week and in the average shop the printer did all the mechanical work. I had reached a point of efficiency where I was supplementing my printing chores by writing brief editorials, especially on the money question. Free silver at the ratio of 16 to one was the big political issue. *The Topeka Capital* was copying many of my editorials. In addition to giving my ego a needed lift, my editorial efforts were responsible for my salary being increased to six dollars a week.

"As a novice editorialist, I found much colorful copy material in Populism. The Populist movement which first came into prominence in the early 1890's was the forerunner of such radical politics as those championed by the late Huey Long and Senator Bilbo of Mississippi. Basically it pitted the 'have nots,' composed of the nation's restless farmers and industrial workers, against the 'haves,' represented by the manufacturing and financial interests of the East.

"Hundreds of colorful characters latched on to the precepts of Populism. They put on a political spectacle that has seldom, if ever, been equalled in contemporary politics. Many of the Populists' most flamboyant oracles were swept into political office. Among these was 'Sockless Jerry' Simpson of Kansas, also referred to as the 'Moses of Medicine Lodge.' Simpson boasted that he was too poor to wear socks while his Republican adversary Colonel Halowell wore silk ones. 'Sockless Jerry' talked himself into Congress.

"Kansas also gave Populism Mary Elizabeth Lease. Mrs. Lease is remembered for her appeal to Kansas farmers 'to raise less corn and more hell.' A torrid orator, Mary Ellen Lease asserted: 'Wall Street owns the country. It is no longer government of the people, by the people for the people, but a government of Wall Street, by Wall Street, for Wall Street.' Mrs. Lease was considered by her followers to be 'The American Joan of Arc.'

"Populism had its distinguished champions outside Kansas. There was Ignatius Donnelly of Minnesota. A great orator, Donnelly's speeches were characterized more by clever sophistry than sound logic. Once lieutenant governor of Minnesota, as a Republican, Donnelly bolted to the Populists when the Republicans declined to support him for a higher office.

"In Colorado, Populism found a staunch adherent in Davis H. Waite, an ardent pro-silver man. Elected governor of Colorado, 'Bloody Bridles' Waite talked of revolution when there was agitation for the repeal of the Sherman Silver Purchase Act. This proposed repeal was seen as a danger to the continued prosperity of Colorado. In the speech that earned him his nickname, Waite said: 'It is better, infinitely better, that blood should flow to the horses' bridles rather than our national liberties should be destroyed.' 'Bloody Bridles' was mainly concerned with the liberty of Colorado to unload tons of Colorado silver on the federal government.

"Populism found rabid support in the South. As a matter of fact, remnants of Populist philosophy are still to be noticed in the impassioned oratory of many contemporary southern politicians.

"Benjamin Tillman, of South Carolina, asked the farmers of his community to rise against the town merchants. He bragged that he was the only man in his state with the brains, the nerve and the ability to organize the common people against the aristocracy. A lot of people must have believed Tillman. He was elected governor of South Carolina and later ran for the United States Senate. Tillman remained a force in South Carolina politics for a generation.

"Georgia also furnished a distinguished Populist luminary, Tom Watson. 'The Sage of Hickory Hill' got himself elected to Congress in a campaign that decried the existence of monopolies and extolled all the virtues of Populism. Later Tom Watson became a United States Senator. In his declining years Watson's politics were notorious for their 'Negro baiting.'

"Populism reached its peak and found its greatest leader in William Jennings Bryan. Bryan was the Democratic Party's most eloquent pro-silver factionist. His meteoric rise in politics began with his election to Congress from Nebraska in 1890. His first legislative diatribes were hurled against the protective tariff. Then he began beating the drum for the unlimited coinage of silver as backing for United States currency. In this he was supported by the silver producing states of Utah and Colorado. Bryan was given financial support by these two states when he campaigned for re-election.

"William Jennings Bryan became the hero of the Populists in 1896 when he made his famous 'cross of gold' speech at the Democratic National Convention in Chicago: 'Having behind us the producing masses of this nation and the world, we will answer their (Wall Street's) demand for a gold standard by saying to them: You shall not press down upon the brow of labor this crown of thorns, you shall not crucify mankind upon a cross of gold.'

"This speech drove the Populists into frenzies of ecstasy and apparently had a similar effect on the Democratic National Convention because the next day Bryan was nominated Democratic candidate for President. The Populists endorsed Bryan for President and then, despite the fact that the Democrats had nominated a vice presidential candidate, picked Populist Tom Watson as their vice presidential choice.

"Bryan campaigned vigorously but failed to defeat McKinley, who campaigned from his home town, Canton, Ohio. Nominated again in 1900, Bryan was again rejected by the American public in favor of McKinley.

"After his second defeat, the 'Great Commoner' went into semi-retirement at his Nebraska home. This became a shrine for his devoted Populist followers. In 1908 Bryan was again nominated for the Presidency but once again was defeated, this time by William Howard Taft.

"With Bryan's political decline, the star of Populism began to descend. Based on no logical principles and championed by demagogues for the most part, Populism which gave such frenzied spirit to national, and especially Kansas, politics began to fade from the national scene. However, as has been pointed out, many of its popular precepts are still to be found in the campaign platforms of political opportunists.

"So you can see what a wealth of material I had to peg my editorials on. Needless to say the *Clifton News* was not a Populist newspaper.

"During my years of apprenticeship on the old *Clifton News* I often had misgivings about the newspaper profession. Like a lot of youngsters from time immemorial, to me the grass always seemed greener on the other side. I found that railroad section hands doing common labor were making much better money than I was. For a while I thought of throwing in my lot with the railroad but I never did. Although I had been doing some writing, it was somewhere around this time that I began to realize that printing was more than setting type in the composing stick and operating the presses. The mechanical phases were merely the tools for conveying the printed word to the readers. Writing was the lifeblood of a newspaper. It was then that I began concentrating on writing.

"I had always been interested in politics and for my age was better informed than many of my elders. I read all the papers that crossed the exchange desk and was steeped in the news and political lore of the time. I sought to express my own ideas by writing. The realization that I could and that many of these ideas were considered worth printing convinced me that journalism had been a wise choice. About this time another event took place which solidified my selection of a vocation.

"The editor of the *Clifton News,* L. A. Palmer, a gifted and courageous writer in the day when libel suits were not uncommon, was to take a two-week vacation and attend a meeting of the *North Central Kansas Editorial Association* in Galveston. Palmer's one column editorials devoted chiefly to exposing the fallacies of Populism and free silver had made him a hero to me. Now he was going forth to meet with other editors of his stature.

"This editorial junket by Palmer and other Kansas greats was an event that deeply stirred my emotions and fixed the destiny of my life. I eagerly awaited the day when a large group of the editors, aboard a Missouri Pacific Special, would pass through Clifton. Charles Stiles, popular and genial Passenger Agent, was to be in charge of the train. I found out that all expenses of the trip, including hotel bills and local entertainment in Galveston, were to be paid by an exchange of advertising. This, I enthused, must be a near approach to the millenium. I could hardly wait until the day when I would see this galaxy of country editors.

"While I had been reading their newspapers on the exchange desk, I had never met them. In the party were such pioneer editors as Del Valentine of the *Clay Center Times;* Gomer Davis of the *Concordia Kansan;* Seward Jones of the *Concordia Blade;* S. H. Dodge of the *Beloit Gazette;* John Q. Royce of the *Phillipsburg Dispatch;* W. C. Palmer of the *Jewell City Republican;*

H. R. Honey of the *Mankato Advocate;* W. H. Nelson of the *Smith County Pioneer;* E. A. Ross of the *Burr Oak Herald,* and many others.

"According to my calendar the event was to be the biggest thing ever witnessed. I shall never forget it, the inexpressible thrill I felt as that train arrived in Clifton in the clear light of morning and disappeared through the deep cut east of town. I started back to the *Clifton News* office taking steps two at a time, fists clenched, repeating audibly: 'I'm going to be an editor, I'm going to be an editor.'

"While these thoughts, arrived at in the unsophisticated mind of a still teen age boy, seemed incapable of any immediate fulfillment, they kept burning themselves into my mind and heart.

"In July 1895, with the thermometer standing at 110 degrees and hot winds blowing from the south, the corn crop was burned to a crisp. L. A. Palmer, the editor of the *Clifton News,* had been out on the streets talking to the farmers and the local businessmen. Their morale was at a low ebb. A dejected Palmer came down into the *News* office, located in the basement under the Bank of Clifton, and told me he would sell me the paper, lock, stock and barrel, for a small down payment. Later *The Kansas City Star* reported that Palmer had sold the paper to his printer presumably to cancel salary obligations. I would like to go on record as saying this was not true. Palmer had never fallen in arrears as far as his payroll obligations were concerned

"I had no idea that a total crop failure had any relation to business conditions and snapped at the opportunity which would make my dream of becoming an editor come true As a down payment I applied twenty dollars I had been able to save from my six-dollar-a-week salary A chattel mortgage was executed on the printing plant and my parents put a mortgage on their home in Clifton for the balance of the cash payment

"I was completely oblivious of what lie ahead This was the

beginning of a fourteen-hour day, twenty-two-year struggle to pay off a series of mortgages on several newspapers.

"Shortly after I purchased the *Clifton News* another very important event occurred in my life. I was married to my childhood sweetheart, Martha Patterson, on October 9, 1895. In the sixty years that we have been together, I have never had cause to regret my choice of a helpmate. When I proposed to Martha I told her some of the dreams I cherished and that to realize these dreams, to make of them something real and solid, would require many years of hard work and perhaps economic hardship. Martha chose to cast her lot with me and we have worked together, side by side, through thick and thin. And, believe me, there were many times when there was much more thin than thick.

"Martha and I set up housekeeping in a six-room house; the rent was six dollars a month. The office rent for that basement under the bank was five dollars a month.

"Corn sold for twelve cents a bushel; wheat for twenty-five cents a bushel; eggs were five cents a dozen; beef cattle went for two dollars a hundredweight and hogs for about the same.

"Clifton's business and professional men lined up in the butcher shop at noon to buy beefsteak for their dinner. Some of them bought ten cents worth; the more conservative with small families bought a nickel's worth of round steak. Tom Tulley, the butcher, would throw in some liver free of charge if requested. I bought ten cents worth of beefsteak for our dinner. Martha chided me for this. The quantity was greater than we could possibly use and Martha, who had been reared in a thrifty Scotch household, could not abide waste. Although I explained that it was a matter of prestige; that I, as the editor of the town newspaper, could not allow people to think I was skimping on my meat purchases, Martha failed to be impressed. I continued

A. Q. Miller, Sr., and Martha Patterson Miller on their wedding day. The outstanding Kansas couple celebrated their sixtieth wedding anniversary on October 9th, 1955.

my extravagant purchases for a while. I'm sure that Martha thought I was a hopeless spendthrift.

"I hired a part time printer for three dollars a week and did the balance of the work on the *News* myself. Income from advertising averaged ten to twelve dollars a week and at that most of the merchants considered it outright charity. My income from job printing ran about the same as advertising. I boasted a subscription list of 500 subscribers at one dollar a year. Western Newspaper Union charged three dollars a week for the five column quarto ready print. The other four pages were hand printed in the *Clifton News* shop.

"All type was set by hand and three to four columns of eight-point type, leaded, was a good day's work of ten hours.

"The first years as editor of the *Clifton News,* because of the crop failure, were pretty bleak and I was often hard pressed to balance the family budget. Few farmers were paying their subscriptions; their buying power was very low and because of this, the merchants cut down on their one- and two-dollar advertisements.

"With corn at twelve cents a bushel I decided to try a promotion scheme and offered to pay fifteen cents a bushel on corn that was brought to the *Clifton News* office to pay for subscriptions. I used a small corn crib belonging to my parents; this was soon overflowing with 250 bushels of corn. I sold the corn for the going price of twelve cents a bushel. In this manner I maintained my subscription price, brought in a substantial number of renewals that I might never have received and, what is most important, drove that wolf a little further away from the Miller's door, at least temporarily. I was quite proud of my first venture into 'high finance.'

"A few days later a very distinguished looking gentleman came into the office and dropped a five-dollar bill on my desk. It was the first five-dollar bill I had ever seen in my life. I stared at it transfixed — completely at a loss for words. I thought that the caller must be offering this sum as a down payment on the purchase of the newspaper. My embarrassment being obvious, the visitor introduced himself. He was A. J. Whitmore, Registrar of Deeds for Washington County, and the five dollars was to pay for a political announcement. This was the very first I knew of a county candidate's obligation to announce his candidacy in the local newspaper. Needless to say I thought it was a very good idea.

"Seeing that I was innocent in regard to the machinations of county politics, despite my editorial writings on national affairs, Whitmore proceeded to give me some very helpful and important advice. He told me that I should go to Washington, the county seat, meet the county officers and other political bigwigs. Before this time such a suggestion would have seemed preposterous. These were big men in the county. What would they possibly want with the acquaintance of a youthful country editor? Whitmore assured me that I was a pretty important person as far as the politicians were concerned and I believed him. I did something that, in that day, was almost unheard of for a small businessman. I hired a livery team for the huge sum of $2.75 for the day, and drove to Washington some twenty miles away. After considerable difficulty, I finally managed to locate the Court House.

Here the first person I met was Cal Morrow, County Treasurer. Cal took me in tow and introduced me to all the county officers who happened to be there on business. In introducing me, Mr. Morrow would say:

" 'This is the new editor of the *Clifton News* and you should subscribe to his newspaper.'

"Thanks to Cal Morrow I raked in a dozen subscriptions at a dollar each and felt more at ease about renting the rig for the trip. Mr. Morrow also earned my undying gratitude. I would have supported him for any office, up to and including President of the United States. Later I did support his candidacy for State Treasurer and was disappointed when he was not elected.

"When I returned to Clifton my head was in a whirl with the grandeur of the personalities I had met at the county seat. I liked politics and had been awakened to the importance of the country weekly in the political life of the community. I was not unaware of the responsibility of the newspaper to the people of the community and was determined that the *Clifton News* would maintain the most rigorous code of ethics as far as its recommendations were concerned. I have always adhered to this standard decided upon well over half a century ago.

"In the fall of 1895 Martha and I took a belated honeymoon and I was able to realize my dreams of attending a meeting of the *North Central Kansas Editorial Association.* On a train, similar to the one which I had so eagerly awaited just a few years before, we were sped to Hot Springs, Arkansas. You can well imagine my complete happiness at this turn of events.

"Unlike so many anticipated experiences, this event was not in the least bit disappointing. The principal address of the meeting was given by Walter Williams, Dean and founder of the University of Missouri School of Journalism. He was one of the first really great men I had ever met. So absorbed was he with the spirit of journalism, that his address removed any lingering doubts I might have had about my chosen profession.

"On returning from Hot Springs, I had my first brush with the law as the result of my terminating a contract for the insertion of a patent medicine advertisement before its expiration. My decision to terminate was based on continual violation of good taste in the copy for the ad. I soon received a threatening letter from the medicine company calling my attention to the fact that I had arbitrarily violated the contract. Rushing upstairs to the bank building, I consulted S. H. Hamilton, a Civil War veteran and lawyer, who had homesteaded a farm adjoining my father's. When I asked him what I should do about the letter, he replied: 'Nothing,' and tossed it into the waste paper basket. He explained to me that the advertising contract called for a weekly insertion to be billed at fifty cents a week. He doubted that the patent medicine firm could afford to hire a lawyer to come all the way out to Clifton, Kansas, to try me for not placing a fifty-cent ad.

"This same S. H. Hamilton was to become quite a power in local politics. A former farmer and lightning rod salesman, he read Blackstone after being appointed Justice of the Peace to replace my father who had resigned on being named to the School Board.

"In 1897 I sold the *Clifton News* for $1300 and bought the *Riley Regent* for $900. I had paid $1100 for the *News* two and a half years before. The equipment of the two newspapers was substantially the same. The revenue from the *Regent* was approximately the same as that of the *News* but I now had two sons, Lloyd, born on July 17, 1896, and Carl Patterson, born on October 30, 1897. With more mouths to feed, I decided, after a survey, that the *Riley Regent* offered a greater potential for growth.

"We moved to Riley and I bought a Jersey cow and a horse and buggy. Clay Center, Manhattan, and Junction City were all within a radius of twenty miles and the horse and buggy was to be used for the trip to these towns, over the rutted dirt roads, on alternate weeks for the purpose of soliciting advertising.

"I suffered from an 'inferiority complex' when it came to selling advertising. Shop keepers and hangers-on used to sit around the large pot-bellied stove in the rear of the store, settling the more vital issues of the day. These merchants did not believe in advertising, placing it in the same category as a charitable contribution. Fortunately, I ran across a publication called

'Success Magazine.' This was filled with stories of inspiration and optimism. It was just what I needed to stimulate my confidence. I saturated my mind with its philosophies until I could approach a merchant, look him squarely in the eye, and make him believe that I had something of importance to sell that he really needed. I was able to convince quite a few of them that a 'dollar donation' would be well placed. On many occasions I traded for merchandise in lieu of cash.

"I received another boost in morale and a practical lesson in psychology from a very colorful young man named James C. Feeley. He came to me with a proposition for a special issue of the *Riley Regent.* This was to be devoted to boosting the town and incidentally writing a 'puff' of the local businessmen to run with their pictures. It was a completely new idea, both to myself and the local merchants. The 'puff,' considered a revolutionary idea then, sold at ten cents a line, cut included. An edition of this nature would violate good taste today unless the 'puffs' were labeled 'advertisement.'

"Feeley had introduced this idea in his own newspaper, the *Sentinel* of Greenleaf, several years before and it had been a tremendous success. He was aggressive, persistent, and gave a well organized sales talk. Riley was the first town where the pictures or cuts were used and the issue was very well received, being widely commented upon by the state press.

"I learned a lot watching Feeley sell the local merchants. It was he who taught me to get the undivided attention of the merchant, even if it were necessary to make a specific appointment. He explained the futility of trying to make sales around the pot-bellied stoves with the audience of townsmen listening in.

"Feeley soon went with the Capper Publications, first selling advertising locally in the *Topeka Capital.* He later went to New York as director of advertising for the entire Capper enterprise. I was told later by Arthur Capper that Feeley used the special edition of the *Riley Regent* as Exhibit 'A' in his presentation to Capper for a job on the *Topeka Capital.* Feeley called on Capper every day for several weeks until Capper 'hired him to get rid of him.'

"Oftentimes in making the horse and buggy junket from Riley to Clay Center, Junction City, or Manhattan, business was combined with pleasure and one or more members of the family went along. I installed a soap box behind the dashboard and operated the reins over the shoulders of my two sons, Lloyd and Carl, then four and two years old. One of my sons blames the slope of his ears on the fact that the reins frequently wound up resting on his ears instead of his shoulders.

"The old township dirt road from Riley to Manhattan followed a course across the Kansas State campus, where the football stadium now stands, until it ran into Poyntz Avenue, the main street of Manhattan. The Junction City road ran through the Fort Riley reservation on approximately the same route as that of the present U.S. Highway 77.

"It was around this time that Carrie Nation of Medicine Lodge, Kansas, became nationally known for her saloon smashing campaign. After throwing rocks through a bar mirror in Kiowa, Barber County, she went to Wichita and smashed up the bar of the Cary Hotel. It was in Wichita that she first introduced her famous instrument of war, the hatchet, which she later carried all over the state in a little black bag. The incident of the Cary Hotel in Wichita received national publicity. This was what Carrie Nation wanted — publicity for her fight against the 'demon rum.' I visited the scene of the shambles in Wichita about two days after it happened and carried away a small piece of a plate glass mirror as a souvenir.

"About ten days later a woman wearing a bonnet and carrying a little black bag came into the office of the *Riley Regent* inquiring for the editor. I immediately recognized my visitor as Carrie

Carrie Nation, ardent, saloon smashing Kansas prohibitionist, with her famous hatchet. Carrie once pinned a rose on the lapel of A. Q. Miller, Sr., when he was editor of the RILEY REGENT.

Nation. Her picture had been in almost every newspaper in the state for days. I was extremely curious to know what she was doing in Riley. After reassuring myself that I had done nothing which might cause her to break the busy hatchet out of its little black bag, I admitted that I was the editor. Carrie smiled, took a rose from her dress and pinned it to the lapel of my coat. This was my first and last decoration for a service of which I was completely unaware. Knowing what Carrie Nation wanted was publicity and that this is what prompted her often unusual actions, I wrote a brief social note about my distinguished caller and charged it up to gratuitous publicity.

"In 1900 I attended my first national political convention in St. Louis and was appointed sergeant-at-arms. As an editor, who by this time was acknowledged to have quite a flair for politics, I was invited to sit in on some inner circle meetings and got an insight into the practical political methods of that generation.

"Upon my return to Riley, I received correspondence from George A. Clark, editor of the *Junction City Republican.* Clark had been elected Secretary of State for Kansas and wished to sell his interest in the *Republican.* I found out that this was a three-way partnership and was not interested in the proposition. As a result of the exchange of correspondence, Clark informed me that a friend of his, George Kyner of Victor, Colorado, was looking for an associate in the publication of the *Victor Daily Times.*

"Victor was located in the heart of one of the nation's leading gold mine districts. I corresponded with Mr. Kyner, who made me a very attractive offer. I sold the *Riley Regent* and bought stock in the Victor Daily Corporation. I was to become business manager and secretary of the corporation. This move was my last adventure outside my native state of Kansas."

CHAPTER III

A Tempestuous Interlude

Unpublished History of The 1903 Cripple Creek Gold Miners Strike

ARRIVING in Victor, Colorado, with his wife, Martha, his two sons Lloyd and Carl, and baby daughter, Enola, born June 18, 1899, A. Q. Miller found the lustry little Colorado city a far cry from towns he had known in the corn belt. Shortly after Miller arrived, the Victor Daily Corporation purchased the *Victor Daily Record* and within a few months acquired two district weekly newspapers. The corporation was booming and so was gold production.

Colorado's Cripple Creek area, one of the most famous gold mining districts in history, had a peak population of 50,000. Cripple Creek proper was comprised of 15,000 inhabitants. Victor, in the very heart of the area, had 10,000 citizens.

A web of electrically operated street cars covered the district, carrying miners to and from the mines. They worked around the clock in eight-hour shifts. The altitude averaged over 9,000 feet and the only crop to be harvested was the miners' payroll. In the peak years, the annual payroll was estimated to be $652,000 and the gold output of the mines $24,000,000. It

Rugged, roaring, Victor, Colorado, as it appeared at the turn of the century when young Miller took over as business manager of the VICTOR RECORD.

Bennett Ave., main street of Cripple Creek, Colorado. Scene of the 1903 struggle for power between the Western Federation of Miners and the Mine Owners Association. There were no victors.

might be noted that Kansas' wheat crop for comparable periods was four times as valuable as Colorado's famed gold production.

Miners were paid on the 10th of each month. This was a field day for the local merchants and saloon keepers. Ninety percent of the checks were cashed in the saloons where the month's bar bills were squared. Poker rooms were very convenient and all too often the miners, when they finally arrived home, hadn't enough money left to pay the family grocery bill.

August 10, 1903, was an historic date in the Cripple Creek area, for on that day the famous Cripple Creek gold miners' strike started.

Labor trouble was not new to the Cripple Creek area. In 1894, after a series of strikes, the eight-hour day went into effect. As a result of this success, the Western Federation of Miners, under the leadership of Ed Boyce, became the strongest industrial union in the United States. Headquarters for the powerful organization were in Denver, Colorado.

Charles Mayer became president of the Western Federation of Miners in 1902. Despite the fact that Mayer was president, it was generally conceded in labor circles that "Big Bill" Haywood, executive secretary, was the power. Big Bill, a staunch socialist of his era, was devoted to destroying "capitalism." In later years, he headed the International Workers of the World, or "Wobblies" as they came to be known. "Big Bill" Haywood decided that the time had come to test the power of the Western Federation of Miners. Cripple Creek, the largest W.F.M. camp in the West, was to be the scene of the contest.

Haywood's initial move was to persuade Cripple Creek's Federation members to allow local officers to act independent of any membership vote. Using these officers as mouthpieces, Haywood began to dictate policies of hiring and firing.

He decided what papers the miners were to read, prepared

"scab" lists and made certain that Teller County officials were friends of the Western Federation of Miners. The mill workers of Colorado City were organized. Charles MacNeill of Standard Mill permitted his employees to join the Western Federation of Miners but steadfastly refused to meet Haywood's other demands.

On August 10, 1903, "Big Bill" Haywood called the Standard Mill's workers out on a strike. As further insurance against operation of the Standard Mill, should MacNeill succeed in obtaining non-union labor, Haywood ordered 3,500 Cripple Creek miners to walk out. Fifty operating mines were brought to a standstill by the strike.

The Mine Owner's Association, an extremely powerly organization, was determined that Haywood's Western Federation of Miners would be stopped once and for all.

There ensued one of the bitterest labor battles of this age. Neither side could lay claim to "Simon Pure" tactics. To date there has never been a complete uncolored history of this troubled period in Colorado's early history. The whole story is best told in A. Q. Miller's own words. After over fifty years, he makes this statement for the records. He holds no brief for either side involved in the half century old contest but believes the story of what happened carries a strong moral lesson concerning the dangers of overriding due process of law and the improper use of military personnel.

"The true story of the Cripple Creek strike never reached the outside world because of a strict military censorship and the arbitrary rulings of Brigadier General Sherman Bell," says Miller. "Governor Peabody had refused to send the military to the Cripple Creek district and put the state to the expense, unless it could be proven that local authorities could not handle the situation. No such evidence was forthcoming as Sheriff Robertson of Teller County and the chiefs of police of both Victor and Cripple Creek contended they could handle the situation. But the mine owners, who had been at war with the Western Federation of Labor, insisted that they wanted to 'clean up the district' of labor influence. Mysterious incidents of violence began occurring over the district, indicating that local authorities could not control the situation. The mine owners told Governor Peabody that if he did not want to put the state to the expense of sending the militia to the district, they would pay the expense. The Governor then ordered the militia to Teller County. This was equivalent to 'hiring out' the militia to the mine owners and subsequent events proved that they so interpreted it.

"Mobs were formed and ran rampant, wrecking union stores and calling on the homes of union men, in an attempt to compel them to leave the district. In some instances, union men were placed aboard trains, taken to the border of the district, and ordered to leave and not return. Mobs, displaying guns and ropes, waited upon the sheriff and chiefs of police of both Victor and Cripple Creek and forced them to resign. Local court officials were given the same treatment and 'friendly' officials were placed in charge so the mine owners and the roving mobs could secure the kind of 'justice' they wanted. These things, of course, were not done by the militia. But they were done by roving mobs while the militia had superseded the local courts and peace officers.

"An outstanding instance of this occurred one day at noon on Bennett Avenue in Cripple Creek. I saw a large crowd assembled in front of a union store and went to see what was going on. A mob was throwing merchandise into the street, wrecking show cases and store fixtures. The store operators and clerks were taken by the mob and marched to the city limits near Mount Pisgah with the warning injunction not to return to the district, even to see their families. Their offense was that they had sold goods on credit to the families of union men who had previously been driven from the district. Military edict stated that no store should sell merchandise to union families on credit. General Bell's orders were that the state would take care of any destitute families.

"So many depredations were being committed in the district, which was ostensibly under martial law, that public opinion revolted and Governor Peabody was flooded with letters and petitions against the lawlessness. Denver newspapers protested the Cripple Creek situation as far as they could get the facts under the strict censorship of General Bell. A sample comment from the *Rocky Mountain News* said: 'Adjutant General Bell should be relieved and removed from command of the troops at Cripple Creek; his mental characteristics are such as to make him an unsafe and dangerous person to hold that position; this has been shown by his conduct since he went to the district, in his disregard of the law and the most ordinary rights of citizens.'

"At the time General Bell was sent to the district, the adjutant general's salary was $1,800, and the Denver papers said the mine owners contributed $3,200 to the fund to make General Bell's salary $5,000, which might have influenced him somewhat in his administratve duties.

"A Methodist preacher in his Sunday morning sermon criticized the militia for not preserving order and criticized the mobs for violating the law. The next day, a mob called at the Methodist parsonage and demanded the preacher's surrender, obviously to take him to what they called the 'bull pen' on Battle Mountain. He refused to surrender and barred the doors of the parsonage. The mob shot through the doors and windows and the parson shot back. Finally, he exhibited a white handkerchief through a window and the battle was over. The pastor was marched to the 'bull pen.'

Lowell Thomas, center, points out object to his son, left, while former Governor of Colorado, Ralph Carr, looks on. The three are standing in front of the old VICTOR RECORD BLDG. *Thomas, son of the Miller's family physician, is a former* RECORD *newsboy. Carr served as a reporter on the* RECORD *before completing his law studies.*

"The militia seemed unable to see these disturbances and breaches of the law. As an eye witness to these events and in an effort to make an objective report of some of the things which took place in the Cripple Creek strike, I am telling this in face of the fact that I had held a prejudice against certain union leaders because of their actions and policies in the past. However, in the case at hand, I was convinced the preponderance of guilt was against the mine owners' organization which had openly boasted that it would 'clean up the district of union men.' This point of view was further confirmed when, at a public mass meeting which resulted in a riot and three deaths, a mine owner told the press: 'There is not room in the Cripple Creek district for both the Mine Owners' organization and the Western Federation of Miners — and I think I know which one will have to leave.'

"It must be understood that the events which I am relating occurred more than half a century ago. Colorado was a comparatively new state. Mining camps attracted many bad characters and had inadequate, loosely enforced, municipal laws.

"Another day I was standing on Fourth Street at the railroad crossing of the F. and C. C. railroad and heard a conversation that amazed me. It was during the strike and non-Union men were working in some of the mines. The engineer in the cab, talking to a railroad man on the ground, said: 'I was told on my trip to Cripple Creek that at a certain curve I would find spikes pulled from the rails and to stop at that point. I did, and avoided a wreck.' This made a good news story and obviously would show the outside world to what lengths the two forces were going. These incidents were taking place all over the district to influence public opinion. Tension between the two groups was very high and no solution to the deadlock was in view. Payrolls were stopped and local merchants and businessmen were suffering. Many stores were forced to close.

"Our newspaper, the *Victor Daily Record,* was criticizing the acts of violence and censoring the militia for not controlling the situation and preserving peace. One Tuesday night at about eleven o'clock, according to a published statement made by George Kyner, the editor, a mob appeared at the rear of the office. Armed with guns and sledge hammers, they forced an entrance to the mechanical department. It was later established that the mob formed at the Dingman cigar store on Third Street and formulated plans for wrecking the newspaper plant to stop its criticism of the military policies in the district. Linotype machines and other office equipment were wrecked. A bullet hole was put in the clock 'just as a reminder.' Mr. Kyner and the night force were marched off to the 'bull pen" on Battle Mountain and slept in a tent that night, with straw for a bedding. Most of the office force of the *Record* was made up of Kansas men, including Mr. Kyner, and at that time consisted of: H. J. Richmond, of Independence, foreman; F. W. and Charles Langdon of Junction City; Chas. Conrad of Salina, pressmen; and Walter Sweet, city editor.

"Before being herded from the plant, Mr. Kyner requested that they leave the metal boy behind. He managed to tell this lad to call me at my home. I was business manager and on the day shift. I was called and informed what had happened. Realizing the importance of getting out some semblance of a newspaper that morning to preserve its legality, I called Charles Conrad at his home and said I would meet him at the office and make a survey of the situation. Mr. Conrad's shift, fortunately, did not start until three o'clock in the morning and we found the mob had overlooked wrecking the Babcock cylinder news press. A few galleys of type had been set and we had plate matter in the office. Here is where my early experience as a printer came in. I set a two-column front page feature story by hand in twelve point, black face, in order to explain to readers what had happened. With the headline, 'A Little Disfigured But Still In The Ring,' we got out a four-page issue of the *Victor Record* that morning.

"I talked to a girl in the telephone office during the night in order to find out what was happening on the outside. We had locked the office doors and pulled down the blinds, as there were reports that the mob might return—and they did, pounding on the doors. I told Mr. Conrad we would leave them the alternative of breaking in the doors if they gained entrance. Later I received a call from one of the telephone operators to tell me that she had heard an officer of the militia tell the men who had been doing the raiding to come back to camp and let the newspaper alone.

"The next morning I contacted an old Kansas friend, Tully Scott, a Cripple Creek lawyer, and told him what had happened. He said the problem was a simple one, as the men had been imprisoned without due process of law and their liberties taken without trial. He immediately used the 'habeas corpus' statute and the men were released, tired, hungry and bewhiskered. Mr. Scott, who had been a western Kansas attorney, became prominent in Colorado politics and was later elected to the Supreme Court of Colorado.

"For several weeks we printed the *Victor Record* on an eight by twelve job press to preserve its legality until repairs could be secured. The *Record* continued to criticize law violations in the district and the inability of General Bell to preserve order. A report reached the *Record* office that General Bell was again looking for Mr. Kyner, the editor, who had gone to Denver on business. I called him at the Brown Palace and informed him of the fact. Mr. Kyner said: 'You tell General Bell that I will return to Victor on the Short Line train at 4:30 if he wants to see me.' There was a crowd at the depot to see what would happen as I met the evening train. I had gone to General Bell's office to tell him that Kyner would be home on the evening train and find out why he wanted to see Kyner. He wouldn't give me an answer but the editor was not molested upon his arrival. Obviously, the General was hearing a lot about public opinion from Denver and out of state newspapers and had decided to soft pedal. At any rate, the *Record* continued to criticize where it thought the public interests were involved and violence tapered off in the district.

"We maintained that our property had been damaged while the district was under martial law and filed a bill with the legislature for reimbursement. Mr. Kyner told me to make out an itemized statement of the physical damage, and we were reimbursed $4,800, by the legislature. In this connection, the *Denver News* said: 'There seems to be little doubt that suits can be maintained against Governor Peabody and General Bell for arbitrary arrests of private citizens.'

"In another article, the *Denver News* commented: 'Adjutant General Sherman Bell should be relieved and removed from command of the troops at Cripple Creek.'

"Relative to the lawlessness and turmoil in the Cripple Creek district, the *Denver Post* stated: 'The situation at Cripple Creek is a reminder of the fact that the President of the United States or the governor of a state have unlimited power in emergencies, but if they exercise it wrongly and it turns out to have been unnecessary, they may be destroyed by their mistakes; there is nothing that the governor of a state or the President tries so earnestly to avoid as the exercise of the power now being used by Governor Peabody; in the case of President Grover Cleveland using this emergency power, the United States mail had to be moved; frankly, it may be doubted that the governor realizes what he is doing.'

John H. White, who began his career as a printer's devil in Clifton, Kansas. His boyhood friend was fellow printer's apprentice, A. Q. Miller. White is shown at his desk in the Colorado legislature.

"At one point in the controversy, District Judge Seeds took jurisdiction and ordered the men in the 'bull pen' released forthwith.

"Following the strike, business in the district deteriorated and the mines never recovered their old production, though there was a period of time when some of the old dumps were worked over because of the increased price of gold. Many buildings were wrecked and moved to towns below. Their salvage value was established by the price of the plumbing fixtures and plate glass."

A short time after the State of Colorado paid reparations to the *Victor Record,* A. Q. Miller sold his stock and returned to his native Kansas. His family was growing and both he and Mrs. Miller decided that the Cripple Creek area, where gambling, drinking and prostitution were the order of the day, was not the proper environment in which to rear a family. A fellow Kansan and boyhood friend, John H. White, whom Mr. Miller caused to be hired by the *Victor Record,* remained, however, to become one of Teller County's most influential and well loved citizens.

John H. White, a New York orphan, reared by W. R. Breugger and John R. Bronson of Clifton, was a printer's devil on the *Clifton Review* at the same time Miller was serving in this capacity on the *News.* The two youngsters, because of their similar "professional status," soon became fast friends. When George Kyner was seeking a circulation manager, Miller told him about John White and two days later he arrived in Victor and started work.

In his capacity as circulation manager, White hired the son of Dr. H. E. Thomas, the Miller's family physician, as a route carrier. The young Thomas is now better known to the nation as Lowell Thomas, explorer, author and commentator. Ralph Carr, later governor of Colorado, was hired as a reporter for the *Record* by White. Carr was persuaded by White to finish his law studies which were the springboard for his successful political career. White later became editor of the *Victor Record,* then was elected to the Colorado State Legislature. He filled the office of County Clerk and Recorder before being named Judge of Teller County.

When the Colorado Midland Railroad ran its last train to Cripple Creek from Colorado Springs, Governor Ralph Carr and world famous Lowell Thomas were reunited with their one-time employer, John H. White, who, then in his late seventies, was a special guest on the final run of an historic rail line.

CHAPTER IV

Belleville and the Belleville Telescope

AN OUTSTANDING NEWSPAPER IN AN IDEAL TOWN

WHEN A. Q. Miller, Sr., and his family returned to Kansas from turbulent Victor, Colorado, Quin was determined that his roaming days were over. Kansas offered as great an opportunity as any other state in the Union and it was home. By now Miller knew there could never be any other profession for him but journalism. He had the money from the sale of his shares of stock in the Victor Daily Corporation. With this, he could buy a Kansas weekly.

Before making any purchase, Quin Miller conducted a personal survey of every county seat weekly in Kansas, those for sale and those not for sale. The *Belleville Telescope,* located in Belleville "At The Crossroads of America" was for sale, and Miller bought it. The *Telescope* offered everything he was looking for in a newspaper and the town was just the kind of place Martha Patterson Miller sought for rearing her family. What kind of town is Belleville?

Belleville, founded on September 25, 1869, is located on gently rolling upland in the middle of a rich and prosperous farming country. It is the county seat of Republic County and an important rail center and shipping point. It is ten miles east of the Republican River and only twelve miles south of the Nebraska state line.

The *Belleville Telescope* was established in 1870. There were but four houses on the townsite at the time the newspaper was launched. First editions of the *Telescope,* printed on a single small sheet, prompted one editor who received an exchange copy to comment editorially:

"I have just seen a copy of the *Belleville Telescope,* a new paper published in Belleville, and I am prompted to say that if it were any smaller, I wouldn't have seen it."

But the *Telescope* flourished and the present paper includes the consolidation of fourteen newspapers that didn't survive.

By 1873 Belleville had become quite an important business center. The main thoroughfare from Hanover, Missouri, connecting with St. Joseph, Missouri, and Denver, Colorado, passed through Belleville, and stages ran daily. A number of substantial business structures had been built and improvements included a city water works. In 1888 Belleville became a second class city. For many years, Belleville was a gateway to the homestead country, to the settlement of which it owes much of its present growth and prosperity.

Today it is operated under the commission form of government with one Mayor and two Commissioners. It has an efficient twenty-four hour police force and fire department, two national banks, a modern municipal library and a beautiful up-to-date 32-bed hospital. A Class A school system consists of a grade school, junior high school and senior high school.

Belleville's present prosperity is largely due to the junction of the two federal trunk line highways: U. S. 36 and U. S. 81.

NEBRASKA
THOMPSON
DESHLER
HEBRON
WILLIAMS
REYNOLDS
HUBBELL
RUSKIN
CHESTER
MAHASKA
WASHINGTON
NARKA
REPUBLIC CO.
HARDY
MUNDEN
HADDAM
SUPERIOR
REPUBLIC
KANSAS
36
WEBBER
CUBA
JEWELL CO.
BELLEVILLE
BRANTFORD
LOVEWELL
81
AGENDA
COURTLAND
SCANDIA
WAYNE
YALMO
HOLLIS
NORWAY
FORMOSO
KACKLEY
CONCORDIA
RANDALL
JAMESTOWN
CLOUD CO.
SCOTTSVILLE
LOOK WHAT YOU GET THROUGH
THE BELLEVILLE TELESCOPE

A. Q. Miller, Sr., played a large part in the establishment of these highways and by so doing, contributed a great deal to the continuing prosperity of Belleville.

The Rock Island Railroad maintains shops in Belleville, one of its important subdivision points. There is a 300-car yard with about 30,000 tons of freight passing through the terminal daily.

Belleville has nine beautiful churches and all businesses and professions are represented in its business district. It is the home of the North Central Kansas Free Fair, a community sponsored event, the third largest of its kind in the state.

In all of this growth and development, the *Belleville Telescope* has played a significant part. When A. Q. Miller, Sr., purchased the *Telescope* in 1904, he began a participation in Belleville civic life that has been continued by his five sons. Merle, who still resides in Belleville, continues active management of the *Telescope.*

Under the Miller banner, the *Telescope* has become Kansas' outstanding weekly newspaper and one of the finest in the country. It has the greatest paid circulation of any Kansas weekly and was the first Kansas weekly to have its circulation audited by the Audit Bureau of Circulation.

Two of three awards won by Kansas newspapers in the 1944 National Editorial Association's annual contest went to the *Telescope:* honorable mention for community service and best editorial. In 1945 it received the best editorial award, first in circulation in 1944, second in Herrich Editorial Award. On and on the honors go — space does not permit a complete tabulation.

A. Q. Miller, Sr., has been asked repeatedly what kind of promotional materials he employs to maintain his outstanding circulation level. Here is what he has to say on the subject:

"Inquiry has been made as to the system used by the *Belleville* (Kansas)*Telescope* in building and maintaining its circulation. Possibly I should first give you a mental picture of our field, population, resources and potential buying power.

"The *Telescope* is published in a typical agricultural section of Kansas where diversified farming and stock raising is practiced. About 70 per cent of the population live on farms and the balance in small towns of from 300 to 500 population. Belleville, the county seat, has a population of 2500, and Republic County a population of 11,654. Using the generally accepted yardstick of four persons to the family, this would make 2,914 homes in the county, which might be considered the 'saturation point' in potential circulation possibilities. During the past year, the *Telescope's* press run averaged 4,238 copies weekly and after deducting left-over and returned copies from news stands, the circulation stood at 4,211. Foreign subscribers and single wraps aggregated 745; exchanges 65, news stand sales 322, office counter sales 55, tear sheets to advertisers 17, miscellaneous newspapers going outside county on border line towns 145. Total deductions for circulation outside county (foreign subscribers, exchanges, advertisers' copies, etc.) leaves a NET PAID circulation inside the county of 3,184—out of a potential possible circulation of 2,914, the number of homes in the county. Allowing for all possible discrepancies and adjustments, the fact that the *Telescope* goes to 270 more families than there are homes in the county is one of those 'Believe It or Not' propositions which the writer is unable to unravel, so let's just call it one hundred percent coverage of the county and let it go at that.

"No high powered circulation methods have been used to build and hold circulation in recent years, though years ago we tried nearly every conceivable circulation plan from commissions, cash prizes, cut rates, automobile contests and trips to contestants. These circulation promotions were costing from $1,000 to $3,000 a year. For more than five years we have used the old fashioned method of trying to print a newspaper covering

BELLEVILLE TELESCOPE AWARDS

First in Circulation Advancement and Second in Herrick Editorial Award, 1944 National Editorial Assn.; First in General Excellence in 1941 and 1942, Kansas Press Assn.; First in Editorial Page, Honorable Mention, Special Edition, 1940, National Editorial Assn.; Second Place, Classified Page, 1938 N.E.A.; First in Circulation Growth, 1938, N.E.A. *Best Kansas Weekly,* First, 1937 and 1940, Second, 1938, Third, 1939 Kansas Press Assn.; Rural News Development Award, 1938 Kansas State College Sigma Delta Chi; First in General Excellence, 1936, N.E.A.; *Best Weekly,* 1936, *Country Home Magazine Award;* Casey's All American Eleven in 1930; Best Editorial, 1945, N.E.A.; Citation of Merit, Ladies Auxiliary V.F.W., 1955; Kansas Industrial Development Commission's Distinguished Service Award, 1951.

the local field and not trying to compete with the metropolitan papers — endeavoring, in fact, to make the paper indispensable. We have been printing weekly from fifty to sixty columns of local and county news. This is possible only by having a competent local news staff and twenty-five alert, well trained, county news reporters, some of whom have been with the paper from fifteen to twenty years, and who are paid for their services. In other words, our aim and goal has been to print an indispensable local newspaper, remembering the old mouse trap story that if the product is good enough eventually the world will make a beaten path to our doorway. As a side light, it might be mentioned that the *Telescope* was established in 1870 when there were but four houses on the townsite and has been under the present management for fifty years.

"There is no particular magic in our plan for maintaining our circulation — it is built on the same business principles practiced by every successful merchant who studies the needs and wants of his customers, the styles of his merchandise, plus superior service. We have been a consistent reader of *Circulation Management Magazine* and other trade publications in search of new ideas and methods for maintaining a high type product for our customers. We believe thoroughly in quality of circulation as well as quantity, because quality circulation represents more buying power — but that is another story.

"How did we find out what our readers wanted? Several years ago we conducted a survey, sending out a double postcard questionnaire, with return card, to 1,000 subscribers, using a cross section of rural and town suscribers. We listed 27 questions on features and news departments carried in the *Telescope* and asked our readers: 'What do you always read?' 'What do you occasionally read?' listing the features in their order of importance, and 'What do you never read?' The answers which came back from these questionnaires gave the paper a very good idea of the kind of 'menu' our customers wanted served. The popular features or departments were: First page, county news, society, editorial, feature stories, sports news, local pictures, cartoons, advertisements, and, believe it or not, many subscribers said they read the classified page first. We carry an average of four columns of classified weekly.

"Now as to the specific method used in maintaining our subscription renewals. It is done by a systematic method of mailing three statements to subscribers whose subscriptions are about to expire. It might be mentioned that the subscription price of the *Telescope* is $2.00 a year and $2.50 outside the state. This subscription statement plan has been used for five years and our readers are now educated (and know) the paper will stop on expiration if not renewed. We maintain a detailed card index list of expirations by months and each month this list is gone over and statements mailed. Four weeks before the subscription expires, each subscriber gets a letter (including a return addressed envelope with no postage required) reminding him that his subscription is about to expire. Two weeks later he gets another letter, reminding him the paper will continue two more weeks and suggesting that the *Telescope* does not want to lose him as a subscriber. If there is no renewal by this time (and this special list of expirations is gradually shrinking) the last letter goes out expressing regret that it will be necessary, on account of postal regulations to drop the name from our family of readers. Our records during the past year show that we have maintained subscription renewals of approximately 95 per cent and that our circulation has increased nearly 700 subscribers on a 'paid in advance' basis. The cost of this mailing service is about $200 a year in postage and paper, not counting the clerical work, and is the most satisfactory and the cheapest circulation method we have ever tried."

CHAPTER V

Good Roads Pioneer

How Two National Highways US 36 and US 81 Came Into Being

DURING the first few years of the twentieth century almost two hundred different types of automobiles had appeared and reappeared. Almost any mechanic, who had the know-how, could put together a pilot model, make extravagant claims of its performance and, capitalizing on the national craze for the horseless carriage, sell a few cars. Many of these "brands" survived barely a year. Take a brief look at some of the names: Apple, Otto, Sebring, Sellers, Zimmerman, Jonz, Westcott. All of these have long since passed into oblivion. And there were those who steadfastly maintained that the entire automobile industry would soon go the way of many of these models.

Almost from the very first, automobile manufacture was centered in the east. There were some manufacturers who built cars in Cleveland and other population centers removed from the east. But Detroit and its environs were recognized as the automobile capital of the nation. It has remained in this position through all the halycon years of automotive development in the United States. When a person living in New York, Chicago, or a similar locale purchased one of these revolutionary contraptions he could find some suitable roads to drive it on. To be sure he might be hailed before a magistrate for annoying horses, or ticketed by a bicycle patrolman for "scorching" down the city streets at ten miles an hour, but at least he could operate his vehicle. There wasn't much point, however, in planning any lengthy trips in the early 1900's because the cars weren't built for it.

By 1910 the automobile had improved; more and more people were becoming interested in owning a car. In this year the nation's multiple manufacturers had produced 181,000 vehicles and the Americans owned and operated almost a half million automobiles. The United States became a nation that wanted to go places but the motorists soon found that they had no place to go. From the south, the middlewest and the west, came the clamor "give us some roads to drive them on and we'll buy your automobiles."

A great number of automobilists, as they were often called then, wanted roads only for joyriding. Detroit was interested in supplying the almost indefatigable demand for motor cars and couldn't be immediately interested in the problem of roads. However, all over the United States there was a solid core of visionaries who saw the automobile as more than a plaything. These men were convinced that they were witnessing a revolution in the nation's transportation methods that was unprecedented even by the dramatic development of the railroad. These men could see that good roads were the next logical step to the expansion of the automobile's use.

In 1910 anyone who ventured outside an urban area in an automobile was considered foolhardy. These were the days when a tourist asking directions might be told:

"Follow the trail along the mountain range south for eighty miles and you'll come to a stick in the fork of a road with a paper tied at the top. Take the rut that leads off to the right."

This is no exaggeration. The above directions were given to Standish Mitchell of the Automobile Club of Southern California who had asked in Albuquerque what would be the best route to Los Angeles. Mitchell's experience was not an isolated incident. Practically all roads outside of townships were paths, at best, in good weather, and hopeless quagmires in bad weather.

In 1910 the new automobile industry had little time for the road problem, a bitter battle was being waged in Detroit as to what method of power was to dominate the automobile. Advocates of steam pointed to the Stanley Steamer, a product of the eccentric Stanley twins, as the quietest, most efficient means of propulsion. Many automotive luminaries could not see anything but the stylish electric. It was almost foolproof—a woman could drive it with ease. Advocates of the electric envisioned a nationwide chain of battery-charging stations that would permit the jaunty electrics to cruise far beyond the limits of a single battery charge. And, in the meantime, the intrepid Billy Durant was busily organizing the automotive dynasty that was to be known as General Motors. While all this was taking place, two Kansans became interested in the automobile. One was to play a dramatic role in the growth of the nation's automotive industry, the other was to become one of the nation's foremost pioneers in the good roads movement.

Walter P. Chrysler, a native of Pottowatomie County, Kansas, who had started as an engine wiper in the Union Pacific roundhouse in Ellis, Kansas, and risen to become manager of the American Locomotive Works at Pittsburgh, quit his $12,000-a-year job and went to work for Buick at half the salary. From here on, his story is legend.

A. Q. Miller, from behind his desk in the offices of the *Belleville Telescope,* became convinced that the success of the automobile would be limited only by the roads available to it.

Initially, he was thinking, as always, of his native Kansas. The automobile could open an entirely new vista to Kansas' rural agricultural population. Trips that were expeditions could become routine. Where families came together only for weddings and funerals, the automobile would make it possible for them to share more adventures and activities.

On June 1, 1911, A. Q. Miller, as delegate from Belleville, attended a meeting at the old National Hotel in Salina to form an association for planning a North-South road across Kansas. The editorial efforts of Miller, and other Kansas journalists, on behalf of better roads was beginning to bear fruit. Much of the public had yet to be convinced, however. The *Topeka Daily Capital,* in a story concerning the Salina meeting of the road-minded delegates, commented: "A North-South wagon road was organized at Salina."

It is also significant to note that the Belleville delegation traveled to Salina, via Junction City, on the Union Pacific Railroad. To travel by automobile would have been inviting disaster. In addition to Miller, the Belleville delegation was composed of two county commissioners: John H. Yale and E. D. Haney; J. C. Price, county surveyor, and J. C. Gurnea. Delegates were present from the eight north-south counties across Kansas and a tentative route connecting all county seat towns was agreed upon.

A budget of ten dollars per county was to be assessed for road dragging and pole painting and all the work was to be voluntary. To assist in dragging the township roads after rains, Fred Quincy, Salina banker, built a road drag and furnished it to the local committee. The pole painting was to enable "travelers" to distinguish between the official North-South road and other township roads and prevent such local directions as: "Just follow the two ruts to the next town."

W. S. Gearhardt, state engineer of Kansas State College, attended the meeting and was authorized to draw a map of Kansas, using a heavy line connecting all county seat towns across the state. This map became the official marker and trade mark. The name adopted was "The Meridian Road" because the newly planned North-South road followed approximately the sixth principal Meridian.

This 1911 meeting in Salina was the beginning of what is now known as the International U.S. 81—Pan-American Highway. It is now paved from Winnipeg, Canada, where it joins Canadian Highway No. 1, to Laredo, Texas, where it meets Mexican Highway No. 4. U.S. 81 is the only highway in the United States whose markers extend uniformly from the Canadian to the Mexican borders.

Between the Salina meeting in 1911 and the completion of U.S. 81, there were many years of untiring and ceaseless effort on the part of A. Q. Miller and other good road pioneers.

The scene in Salina where the humble beginning of U.S. 81 took place was being repeated in many other parts of the nation as more and more good road boosters began their organizations. Almost all of the major U.S. highways which we know today were planned in the first fifteen years of the century. At that time, they were called "paper roads" and many people thought they would never get out of the "paper" stage. They didn't know the determination of the highway devotees.

Even before the 1911 meeting in Salina, the advocates of better and more durable roads got an insight into the technical difficulties that would be encountered, as well as the apathy on the part of great numbers of the public. In 1904 Salina County commissioners authorized construction of a one-mile cement experimental road. It crumbled away in a few months because no one knew how to mix cement so it would stand up under traffic.

W. S. Gearhardt's "Meridian" map of Kansas was reproduced on the stationery of the Association formed at the Salina meeting. Metallic markers incorporating the "Meridian" trade mark were used to define the route. This is one of the earliest known instances of the use of metallic signs to identify a highway route.

Needless to say, in 1911 there was no Kansas Highway Department. It can readily be seen what a gargantuan task faced the organizers of the Meridian Road, embryo of U.S. 81. Neither state nor county had the right to build roads. The township board was the only governmental unit having legal authority to construct roads. All too often, their vision did not extend beyond the township limits or, at best, the local market center. This, too, was the day of narrow wooden bridges, undrained roads and tin culverts.

To A. Q. Miller, who had been elected treasurer of the Meridian Road Association, fell the unenviable task of getting township cooperation and raising funds for improvements where township cooperation was lacking. Miller gave unstintingly of his time and effort and before too long the Meridian Road became a reality. Uniform metallic road signs and painted poles announced to adventurous motorists the best North-South route across Kansas.

Now the Association sought national recognition for its new trans-state road. In this day, the bible of the motorist was the Automobile Blue Book. Recognition of the route by publishers of the Blue Book and inclusion of mileage and supplemental data within its covers would assure use of the Meridian route by hardy interstate travelers.

To gather data for the Blue Book, it was necessary to log the road and accurately plot the mileage between the various towns. A Blue Book representative accompanied the logging party. In September of 1912, just sixteen months after its first Association meeting in Salina, the logging trip got underway. In a Winton Six, furnished by S. E. Jackman of Minneapolis, Kansas, an enthusiastic worker for the Meridian Road Association, the logging party charted the route from Chester, Nebraska, to South Haven, Kansas.

As the North-South Meridian Road began to be projected into other States, as a part of a national highway, Belleville, in its geographic center, became a key city. On March 21, 1913, A. Q. Miller was elected secretary-treasurer of yet another highway association. The newly planned east-west highway which was to intersect the already inaugurated north-south highway at Belleville, placing this bustling Kansas community at the crossroads of America.

Taking note of the Belleville meeting, the *Topeka Daily Capital* said: "One of the most active bunch of good roads boosters in Kansas met at Belleville and organized another wagon road across the state." Once again the reference to a wagon road indicated that there was still a certain amount of skepticism regarding the activities of Kansas' pioneer highway champions.

The new association was organized to mark an east-west route across a northern tier of Kansas counties and form a direct connection between St. Joseph, Missouri, and Denver, Colorado. D. E. Watkins of Topeka, as head of the Kansas Sunflower Automobile Club, had made a tour of northern Kansas and suggested an east-west routing through this section of Kansas. When A. Q. Miller was informed of Watkins' suggestion, he swung into action. Belleville was proposed by Miller as the place for the initial meeting and he took care of all the details.

Delegates present were from practically all the northern counties as well as officials of the Rock Island Railroad. Officers were elected to head the new organization. They were: Dr. C. W. Cole of Norton, President; Charles F. Travelute of Marysville, vice president; and A. Q. Miller, of Belleville, secretary-treasurer. Once again, Miller found himself in the "work-horse"slot.

A tentative route for the new highway was agreed upon. For many miles this paralleled the Rock Island Railroad and was named the Rock Island Highway. Later the road was merged into the Pike's Peak Ocean to Ocean Highway and when official Federal markers were adopted became known as U.S. 36. At the close of the meeting, the delegates voted to log and map the route from St. Joseph to Denver and authorized A. Q. Miller as secretary-treasurer to raise necessary funds and take charge of the tour. Quin Miller again was spearheading the functional operation of a program destined to give the nation one of its most important trans-continental motor routes.

It should be pointed out that the only remuneration received by these pioneers for better roads was the satisfaction of seeing their faith in the future of the motor car justified. So strong was their belief that they gladly devoted days and months to their promotional efforts, even though this time had to be taken from the jobs and businesses that furnished a livelihood for them and their families.

At the time the initial meeting was held in Belleville nobody had ever traveled the newly proposed route, knew the mileage or even where it was located on the ground. Actually the new artery was a series of disconnected township roads the entire width of the state. The St. Joseph Commerce Club offered to finance one car, an Overland 70, owned and driven by Dr. Stevenson. The St. Joseph Auto Club designated and financed the pilot car, a Kissell, owned and operated by H. J. Leslie.

On the morning of September 21, 1913, the official party set out from the Rubidoux Hotel in St. Joseph. It was composed of Governor George H. Hodges, D. E. Watkins, W. S. Gearhardt, A. Q. Miller and an official from the Blue Book Corporation. Four days later the two car convoy arrived in Denver, hub deep in mud, at two o'clock in the morning. The highway was officially logged and mapped, recorded in the Blue Book and started on its way to national fame.

During one of the muddy, rainy days when the cars were

(Left to right) – Governor George H. Hodges; A. Q. Miller, publisher BELLEVILLE TELESCOPE; *D. E. Watkins, (retired Manager Calif. Auto Club) Secretary-Manager Kansas Sunflower Auto Club; H. J. Leslie, representative St. Joseph Chamber of Commerce; J. R. Edwards, Chicago, representative Automobile Blue Book, leaving Robidoux Hotel, St. Joe, on logging trip. (A. Q. Miller, Secretary-Treasurer and Manager of tour.)*

slipping over the almost impassable ruts with their wheels spinning madly, the Blue Book man sitting next to Governor Hodges continued calmly to plot his mileage. Governor Hodges remarked that with all the fruitless wheel spinning the mileage readings must be way off and that he, for one, would hate to have to depend upon the Blue Book data. His fears were soon assuaged by the driver who pointed out that the speedometer was connected to the front wheels, which didn't spin, so the mileage readings would be accurate.

Because Governor Hodges was a member of the entourage, the highway logging trip was made a festive occasion for many of the towns along the route. Flags were flown, schools were dismissed and children lined up along the streets to greet the Governor. Some of the towns even staged band concerts at important intersections.

Local chambers of commerce furnished pilot cars to guide the party between towns and thus fix the official route. Mayor E. L. Johnson of Belleville drove his new Marmon car to Marysville to escort Governor Hodges to Belleville. Halfway between Belleville and Marysville the car was stalled in the mud and did not arrive until the next morning. On the return trip the Mayor's car was again bogged down and did not reach Belleville for two days. This will give readers an idea of what Kansas roads were like half a century ago. This condition was by no means peculiar to Kansas, practically every state in the Union was faced with the same situation to one degree or another.

A. Q. Miller's interest and participation in the new east-west highway did not end with the establishment of the route across Kansas. Along with other good roads promoters, he soon saw that national highways would result only by cooperation between many states and communities. The work done in Kansas was just the start. His discernment of the situation was verified before many months had elapsed. At this juncture in the development of the Pike's Peak Ocean to Ocean Highway, routing problems began to arise, as they did with every pioneer highway development. It was decided to route the young highway from St. Joseph to Colorado Springs, instead of Denver. Kansas City and Denver already had a working agreement for the routing of automobile travel between Kansas City and the Rocky Mountains and all projected roads up to that time were laid out between those two metropolitan centers. Neither St. Joseph nor Colorado Springs approved that routing and decided to link their interests in developing a shorter and more direct route across Kansas. This decision and subsequent incidents marked the destiny of the road as an independent national highway.

The Colorado Springs Chamber of Commerce played a major role in the rapid development of this route across the country, which until now, has been unprinted history. Without the financial aid of both Colorado Springs and St. Joseph, it is doubtful if this road would ever have attained the prominence of a national highway. A. W. Henderson, former secretary of the Colorado Springs Chamber of Commerce, was released by his association to devote most of his time over a period of years to the development of this artery as an independent route across the United States. He made several trips to New York and California to perfect his plans. The National Lincoln Highway (U.S. 30) having adopted the name of the Colorado State Lincoln Highway and routed its way from Colorado through Cheyenne, Colorado Springs became furious and sought an eastern connection. This, logically, brought her to St. Joseph, which likewise was looking for a friend.

Upon the occasion of a Kansas road meeting at Norton, Mr. Henderson of Colorado Springs and Judge J. W. Dean of Aspen, Colorado, attended the meetings, having had instructions from Colorado Springs to find an eastern outlet for tourist traffic. They explained later that their Kansas objective was Kansas

David E. Watkins, one of Kansas pioneer good road boosters. Recently retired as secretary and general manager of the California State Automobile Association, Watkins has devoted a lifetime to the nation's motorists. Under his direction the CSAA grew from a few hundred members in 1913 to over 280,000 in 1953.

City, where they had appointments with Judge J. M. Lowe of the Santa Fe Trail (U.S. 50) and Charles M. Harger of the Golden Belt (U.S. 40) hoping to persuade them to reroute their roads to Colorado Springs instead of Denver. Their stop at Norton proved fruitful.

The Belleville delegation took a train back home and persuaded the Colorado contingent to ride back to Belleville over the Rock Island Highway (U.S. 36) in A. J. White's Buick car. Here they boarded a Rock Island train for St. Joseph, arriving there on the date of the annual meeting of the St. Joseph Auto Club.

This trip resulted in a coalition of interests, which later proved mutually advantageous. Immediately, St. Joseph and Colorado Springs joined in calling a meeting at St. Joseph on March 17, 1914, to merge all local road interests into a national highway. The result of this meeting was the merger of the old Lincoln Highway in Colorado, the Rock Island Highway in Kansas and the White Cross Trail in Missouri.

A. Q. Miller presided at the significant St. Joseph meeting on March 17, 1914. Committees were appointed, including a marker committee, and the road was officially named the Pike's Peak Ocean to Ocean Highway, symbolizing Pike's Peak on the one hand and the two oceans on the other. More than one thousand metallic markers with the above trademark were erected along the highway. National officers elected at the St. Joseph meeting were Charles F. Adams, Chillicothe, Missouri, president; A. Q. Miller, Belleville, Kansas, vice-president, and A. W. Henderson, Colorado Springs, secretary-treasurer.

This organization became one of the most efficient and best financed groups of its kind in the country. A general manager was employed and through memberships and assessments a budget of more than $40,000 a year was provided to promote and publicize the road, paint poles, erect markers and produce advertising folders and maps. Colorado Springs and St. Joseph, realizing the importance of an independent highway and the revenue that would result from future traffic, each contributed $5,000 a year to the budget.

An outstanding public relations achievement of A. W. Henderson was that of securing a two-page story in *Motor Age,* the nation's leading automotive publication at that time. The story complete with maps featured the Pike's Peak Ocean to Ocean Highway from New York to California. A solid black line indicated the routing from New York to Salt Lake City, Utah. Two dotted lines were used to show routes to California; one to Los Angeles, the other to San Francisco. Henderson, by using the dotted lines, clearly indicated that the western terminus of the highway was undetermined.

When this issue of *Motor Age* was distributed in California, the Pike's Peak Ocean to Ocean office was flooded with letters and telegrams from San Francisco and Los Angeles bidding for the western terminus of the highway. Delegates from California attended the annual meeting at St. Joseph, making bids for their respective cities. Henderson's subtle strategy had worked out beautifully.

The Pike's Peak Ocean-to-Ocean Highway needed a western terminus but wanted to locate that gateway in a Pacific Coast town that would promise full cooperation in the routing of east bound traffic. San Francisco was finally selected as the city in which the new trans-continental highway would terminate.

As U.S. 36 and U.S. 81 projected east and west, north and south, from the state of their origin, A. Q. Miller's arduous work on their behalf increased rather than diminished. He took a very active part in the national associations for the promotion of both highways. Much of the literature, several of the guide books and brochures promoting the young highways, was printed in the job shop of the *Belleville Telescope,* always at cost and quite frequently at a loss. Miller's extensive travels to meetings of the various associations were paid for out of his own pocket.

The largest obstacle that had to be overcome by the early day good roads pioneers was intersectional rivalry and the activities of selfish interests. Too many individuals and communities were thinking narrowly. Miller recognized almost at once that no successful trans-continental highway could possibly travel a saw-tooth route just to please the many communities that wanted it to pass through their borders. The old axiom of the greatest good for the greatest number had to be considered in highway development. It is a tribute to these pioneers, often called upon to exercise the wisdom of Solomon, that, although temper and feelings ran high at times, there were practically no long lasting feuds resulting from the routing of the highways.

Sometimes the decision of the federal authorities when they entered the picture with grants of funds were a little hard to take but, nevertheless, the decrees were accepted. An example of one such decision was the final routing of U.S. 36 to Denver instead of Colorado Springs. This, despite the years of effort on the part of Colorado Springs, through the indefatigable A. W. Henderson, and the expenditure of huge sums of money. Henderson, an ill man, literally died in the saddle carrying on the work of promoting the east-west highway. When the Federal Bureau of Public Roads and State Highway officials met in Chicago to distribute Federal markers the routing went to Denver. This was believed to be in the best interest of the nation.

One encroachment on his beloved Belleville A. Q. Miller decided was not in the public interest and he fought it successfully. This had to do with the slogan: "Cross Roads of America." In 1925 Salina, Kansas, sought to appropriate this name to itself in view of the fact that the Victory Highway and the Meridian Road intersected there. Miller's indignation was great and in the good natured battle that followed Miller presented evidence that he had copyrighted the slogan at the time the Pike's Peak Ocean to Ocean Highway was organized. Salina retired from the battle gracefully, revising its slogan to read: "Where North Meets South and East Meets West."

A. Q. Miller, President Emeritus of the U.S. 36 and U.S. 81 Highway Associations, in recent years has received many tributes for his work in fathering the two great national highways. Perhaps one of the finest was an editorial in *The Denver Post,* May 23, 1949.

"It was back in 1913 that a group of road boosters in Kansas got together and formed an association to get improvements for the route now known as U.S. 36. One of that group, and probably the strongest booster of all, was A. Q. Miller, owner of the *Belleville Telescope.*

"Other boosters for U.S. 36 became discouraged, but not Mr. Miller. Over a period of more than thirty years he probably wrote more articles about '36' than have been written about any other road in the world. Gradually, bit by bit, the road was improved. Finally only the stretch in Colorado remained without a hard surface.

"Mr. Miller kept right on plugging. He visited Colorado frequently. He enlisted supporters for '36' in Denver and other Colorado towns. He wrote guest articles for the *Post.* In Elwood Brooks, Denver banker, he found a kindred spirit as far as road promotion work was concerned.

"At last Colorado's section of '36' has been surfaced. Friday and Saturday there was quite a celebration. One important figure was absent, however. Mr. Miller, who had just gone through a strenuous U.S. Chamber of Commerce election campaign, was advised by his physician not to come to Denver for the 'road doings.'

"So the father had to miss the christening but there were plenty of godfathers and if you had asked them, every one of

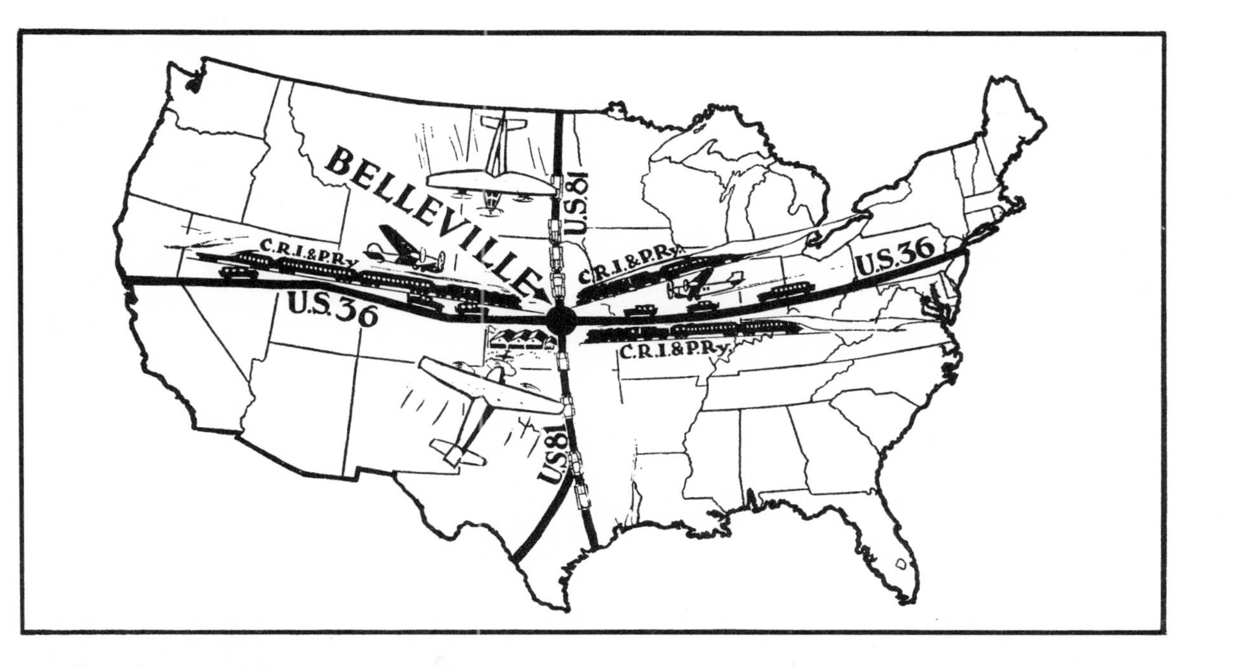

In the early years of the twentieth century the two national highways, shown above, were started in Kansas by a small group of good road pioneers. At that time they were somewhat skeptically hailed as paper roads. Intersecting at Belleville, home of the BELLEVILLE TELESCOPE, *the two national arteries establish Belleville's claim of being at "The Cross Roads of America."*

them would have said that the man principally responsible for keeping the Highway 36 idea alive during the tough years was A. Q. Miller, the man who never gave up."

Two years previous to the *Denver Post* editorial, A. Q. Miller who for years had been president of the U.S. 81 Highway Association decided to step down. The association elected Lynn D. Hutton to succeed Mr. Miller. An excerpt from Mr. Hutton's speech of acceptance paid tribute to the retiring president:

"I appreciate the honor you have conferred upon me. I most sincerely regretted to hear that Mr. A. Q. Miller, our distinguished President, felt that he could no longer serve in this capacity. To me he has been the principal motivating force in this organization as long as I have been associated with it. Your very thoughtful act of making him President Emeritus of this organization gives me great pleasure. It recognizes a great builder, a fine leader and, while relieving him of many of the arduous tasks incident to the active presidency, retains him in an advisory position where his wise counsel still will be valuable to the organization with which he has been associated for over 36 years. I congratulate the U.S. 81 Association for its wisdom in retaining Mr. Miller in this capacity."

A. Q. Miller has lived to see his dreams of national highways fulfilled. What scoffers referred to so often as "paper roads" are now a reality. A great debt is owed Mr. Miller and his fellow pioneers who weren't content to sit back and "let George do it."

There is no minimizing the large contribution played by the *Belleville's Telescope's* persistent and erudite editorials on behalf of good roads. The small but eloquent voice of this outstanding newspaper was heard throughout the nation. But Miller did more than write about roads, he got out from behind his desk and worked for them. He was a familiar figure at every good roads meeting in the middle west and other parts of the nation. He was the spark plug that kept the campaign alive even though others were temporarily discouraged. A. Q. Miller had faith and he has lived to see that faith justified.

CHAPTER VI

Kansas Flood Control

THE FIGHT FOR ADEQUATE UPSTREAM CONTROLS

RIVERS, by the very nature of the elements, must necessarily overflow from time to time. History has recorded catastrophic floods from the very beginning of civilization. In the United States the damage caused by floods increased with the westward expansion and development of the nation. Flood plains which were designed by nature to receive the tempestuous overflow of the nation's rivers began to be inhabited. Floods, which were once harmless, began to take an increasing toll in life and property.

Basically, in dealing with the flood hazards, two alternatives were presented; flood plains must be by-passed as areas of agricultural and urban development or some man-made attempt must be made to control the flood problem. If flood plains had been by-passed in the westward expansion of the nation then some of the richest agricultural states would today be nothing more than wide expanses of federal territory. Uninhabited, undeveloped, because of the certain knowledge that sooner or later rivers would overflow their boundaries and roll unchecked over these fertile areas. Quite logically, intrepid American pioneers chose to develop these rich middle-western plains and as their farms prospered, towns and cities came into existence to supply them with the commodities necessary to their existence and to process the rich yield of foodstuffs that were necessary to the life of this great nation.

Kansas is typical of the middle western states which have a large urban population and great agricultural enterprises. One serves the other and the mutuality of interests is clearly recognized by both segments of the population. Yet there is one subject on which there has been a notable lack of accord — flood control. One can take the history of Kansas' flood control and with it, trace the history of the nation's flood control. The great strides that have been made in the adequate handling of the nation's flood control problems are attributable, in a large measure, to the efforts of Kansans. Notable among these has been A. Q. Miller who, for well over half a century, has fought for intelligent conservation and flood control measures through the pages of his newspaper, the *Belleville Telescope,* and by actively participating in active public relations and legislative programs for the betterment of flood control measures. The principles for which A. Q. Miller fought have now come to be recognized as the basic essentials of adequate flood control by most authorities on the subject. This recognition has not been brought about overnight.

Let us trace the history of flood control in the United States and then tie this history in with Kansas, bearing in mind that Kansas is representative of most of the agricultural middle west. It will be seen, readily, how significant the contributions of A. Q. Miller and other advocates of overall flood control have been.

In 1824 the Corps of Engineers was authorized to undertake projects designed to improve and maintain the navigability of the nation's rivers. At this time water routes were all important and the insurance of adequate channel depth was vital to the transportation system. So that is how the Corps of Engineers got into the act originally. In a sense, insurance of navigability seemed to be their major interest long after the rivers had lost their importance as arteries of transportation.

It was not until 1850 that the Corps of Engineers was requested to concern itself with flood control. In this year Congress authorized a survey of the Mississippi River. Included in this investigation was to be recommendation of a plan to insure against the flooding of the river. This is the first mention of flood control in connection with the Corps of Engineers until the twentieth century. The program of the Corps of Engineers dealt mainly with the engineering needs of the federal government; navigation improvements, expansion of roads and railroads, and mapping of territories.

Various federal commissions were created to deal with flood problems. One of these was the Mississippi River Commission in 1879. This was significant because it was the very first acknowledgement that the federal government had a responsibility in flood control problems too large or too complex for the state or local governments. It was the first acknowledgement by the federal government that floods could affect the welfare of the entire country to some degree.

In 1908 Congress established the Board of Engineers for Rivers and Harbors. While this body was still concerned with navigation, it shortly found itself immersed in related flood problems when hydroelectric power came under consideration in survey reports. In 1917 the first Flood Control Act was passed. This provided that federal laws relating to rivers and harbors should concern themselves with flood control. So gradually the federal government began to assume a responsibility for controlling the rampages of the nation's rivers.

Now came another question in regard to flood control measures. Who was to bear the expense of such projects? The first mention of assessing costs to the communities benefitted was made in the Rivers and Harbors Act of 1920. However, flood control activity along the Mississippi in 1928 was undertaken almost entirely at the expense of the federal government. But the Act authorizing the program for 1928 along the Mississippi's alluvial valley provided that for flood control works above the alluvial valley or along the tributaries, one-third of the cost should be borne by local interests and these same local interests should provide rights of way and make further provision for maintenance and operation.

Flood control projects undertaken by the Corps of Engineers as depression work relief projects caused a change of thinking in regard to the responsibility of financial participation by local interests. These projects were responsible for the recognition of flood control as a federal responsibility and the passage of the first general Flood Control Act of 1936. In this Act of 1936, Congress pointed out that flood control on navigable waters or their tributaries is a federal responsibility in the interest of the general welfare.

With federal recognition of its flood control responsibility, it would seem that all should proceed smoothly. Such was not the case. Now the question raised was what type flood control program should be pursued. Let's look at the Kansas picture.

Kansas, like many other middle western and southern states, for years had been plagued with spring floods. These varied in intensity through the years but over a period of time had been responsible for loss of innumerable lives and millions of dollars in property and land damage. Attempts had been made to control the nation's more turbulent rivers but the control exercised was not designed or intended to prevent floods at their source.

Back in 1933 when Henry Woodring was Assistant Secretary of War under President Franklin D. Roosevelt, the President announced a flood control program for Kansas as a part of a federal works project. The project called for the building of $75,000,000 Kiro Dam on the Kaw River, west of Topeka. This project had been prepared in the Kansas City Division Office of the U. S. Corps of Engineers by Captain Theodore Wyman and approved in Washington. When the announcement was made of the Kansas flood control project by the President, the people of the state were up in arms and they conducted one of the bitterest fights the state had seen since the battle over statehood.

Citizens of towns and communities living on tributaries of the Kaw River took the position that this did not constitute a valid flood protection program for the state and if such a program went through, it would kill future flood control programs on the tributaries. These tributaries of the Kaw River were the Republican, Smoky Hill, Saline, Solomon and Blue rivers. A mass meeting was called at Salina, October, 1933, by the Salina Chamber of Commerce and delegates from communities along all the tributaries attended to formally register their protests.

This meeting formed what was known as the Kaw Valley Basin Flood Control Association with the announced purpose of developing an alternate for the unpopular and impractical Kiro Dam proposal. Frank Merrill of Ellis was elected President, Charles Breen of Salina, secretary-treasurer, A. Q. Miller was designated public relations officer and authorized to prepare a brief, with engineer's maps and blueprints, setting up locations, costs and other data, including possibilities of irrigation, soil conservation and the production of electrical energy where feasible.

A firm of private engineers, Paulette and Wilson, was employed by the various local communities in preparing their plans and these were incorporated into a master plan. A. Q. Miller personally took this detailed master plan to Washington and filed copies with the War Department, the Kansas Congressional Delegation and the National Resources Board. The latter agency had the power to approve public works projects.

Miller, whose vociferous *Belleville Telescope* had sounded the clarion when the ill-fated Kiro Dam proposal was originally announced, continued his efforts. *Telescope* editorials on the danger and inadequacy of the Kiro program were reprinted in other state papers and read into the Congressional Record. Miller's paper was joined by the major press of the state. Washington was flooded with telegrams, petitions, letters and newspaper clippings. The government made a strategic withdrawal. General Markham, Chief of Staff, was asked to re-study the Kiro Dam project and delivered an official report declaring the Kaw River project unsound. He stated in his report that the benefits of the original proposal were not commensurate with the costs and property loss. Captain Theodore Wyman, who designed Kiro Dam and was largely responsible for pushing it through, was transferred to Los Angeles. Public opinion had won the skirmish and the principle of tributary control was established. The big battle, however, was not yet won.

An excerpt from a report by A. Q. Miller to the Kaw Valley Basin Flood Control Association gives a clear indication of the struggles that were ahead:

"Your representative believes that any plan which is developed for the Missouri River and the Kaw, will take into consideration the tributaries as well. But the fight is not yet won. In the final analysis we are faced with the problem of navigation on the Missouri and Mississippi rivers, and the keeping of these channels open for barge service the year round. This is the national program and the only basis on which the tributaries can get 100 per cent federal aid. Our brief supporting data sets out that we can impound on the tributaries 5,000,000 acre feet of water at approximately one-half the cost of the Kiro project, and release this water, as needed, into the Missouri River at Kansas City, thereby meeting the government requirements as programmed by the Army engineers.

"At the present time we are endeavoring to get an unbiased study of the whole plan by engineers, with government authority, and have high hopes of accomplishing this. In the meantime we have practically the solid support of the Kansas congressional delegation behind our unified plan. The White House and Mr. Ickes have been quoted as favoring a broad study of the entire Missouri Valley and its tributaries, dealing with the problem as a whole, rather than piecemeal. This fits exactly into our program, as presented at Washington.

"But the fight is not yet won. We have got to stay on the job and see it through and not lose by default the ground already gained. Any plan which would establish the principle of flood control and navigation and not include the tributaries would eliminate them permanently from 100 per cent federal aid. Thereafter, the tributary project would come under the classification of 30/70 federal aid. Hence the necessity of waging the fight to stay in the program."

While Washington recognized the logic of the Kansas plea for tributary control as an effective means of preventing or materially reducing the annual flood toll, the War Department still did not have the necessary authority. Finally, after the Republican River flood in June of 1935, which cost one hundred lives and $10,000,000 in property, Congress amended War Department authority to cover flood control as well as navigation.

Despite efforts to educate local and state governments on the importance of tributary control, various detrimental proposals kept cropping up. A. Q. Miller and his fellow workers had to remain continually on the alert to combat these forces. Typical of Miller's editorial effectiveness is the following from the *Belleville Telescope* of October 28, 1937.

"A flood control committee representing five states met at Kansas City last week and approved what they called a 'Flood Control Program for the Lower Mississippi River.' This report and recommendations will be transmitted to the National Resources Committee and to President Roosevelt.

"F. H. Fowler, water consultant for the Mississippi river basin, attended the meeting in an official capacity and endorsed the program, which proposes two super-reservoirs located 50 miles apart on the Republican and Blue rivers, to cost $63,000,000. This is offered as 'a flood control program for Kansas.'

"Frankly, the program is designed only for flood protection on the Lower Kansas River and for navigation and flood control on the Lower Mississippi River. Mr. Fowler, Washington representative, is frank to admit that the program is for the Lower Kansas River and has as its main objective protection for the Lower Mississippi. The *Kansas City Star* quotes Mr. Fowler as saying: 'The proposed project would solve the flood problem of Kansas City, Lawrence and Topeka, and it would help materially in preventing floods on the Lower Mississippi.'

"This is the flood control program Kansas would get from the federal government, according to Mr. Fowler. Such a preposterous proposal is a joke and will never get the approval of the people of Kansas and the *Telescope* predicts it will never go through.

"For more than two years, at stated intervals, Army engineers have reported favorably on the Milford dam site on the Republican River, and on the Tuttle Creek site on the Blue River, adjacent to Manhattan — and nothing has ever been done about it, because the proposals have been so ridiculous that they have not inspired public confidence in their practicability. If Kansas were to accept as her allocation $63,000,000 for flood control and have it wasted on two reservoir sites within 50 miles of each other, the state program for soil erosion, water conservation and flood protection would not only be crippled, but seriously delayed, if not entirely defeated.

"Engineering surveys and records show that a similar reservoir on the Republican could be constructed at Scandia, impounding an equal amount of water at a cost of $15 per acre foot, as against $23 an acre foot for the Milford site. The total cost of the Scandia reservoir would not exceed $9,000,000 as against $35,000,000 for the Milford project.

"Nothing was said at the Kansas City meeting about flowage rights, acreage and right of way. The federal government requirement has always been that local communities or benefit districts assume this item of expense, a stumbling block on all large projects. Kansas City, Topeka and Lawrence have thus far been unable to meet the flowage right and acreage stipulation of the federal government to secure their levees. In this connection it is reasonable to suppose that the Milford and Tuttle Creek communities would be unable to finance their part of such a huge program, even if the plan secured Washington approval.

"Mr. Fowler and the Army engineers seem to lose sight of the fact that Kansas is 400 miles long and 200 miles wide, comprising many watersheds and streams which subject millions of acres of farm land and city property above the Kaw to flood menace. Likewise, the state has the very important problem of soil erosion, water conservation, restoring water tables, irrigation and rural electrification, which are offered to the country as a national program. If Kansas should accept and waste the money allocated to the state on two super-reservoirs to aid navigation on the Lower Mississippi and provide flood control on one stream, it might be a cold day before the state received additional funds toward dealing with the more pressing problems as outlined in a national plan already offered the several states.

"Water committees may continue to meet in Kansas City and pass resolutions till doomsday, sponsoring a program which is foreign to the real interests and needs of Kansas, but it will be time and energy wasted until they visualize and understand the Kansas picture and the true Kansas problems.

"The fundamental principles involved in this question were debated and tried out in this state several years ago... It would be presuming too much on the patience of the people of Kansas to ask them to thresh over a lot of old straw."

Today there is still a difference of opinion between the advocates of downstream and tributary flood control methods. It is doubtful that this controversy will ever be completely resolved. Due to A. Q. Miller's efforts on behalf of the Kansas tributary spokesmen, the nation is now prosecuting a more well balanced flood control program. The staunchest adherents of the downstream or big dam school have come to realize that there is considerable merit to the tributary or upstream planners.

A. Q. Miller has repeatedly pointed out that any national flood control program must take into consideration the principle of the greatest good for the greatest number. Violation of this precept is what has hamstrung the overall flood control program. There has been a lack of harmony between government agencies as well as different communities. Miller continues his efforts to eliminate these frictions. Current editorials in the *Belleville Telescope* beseech citizens to consider each proposed flood control project in the light of its relation to the overall picture and not from a strictly regional or local interest point of view.

There are two government agencies reflecting the two major programs of flood control. The United States Department of Agriculture upholds the theory of upstream engineering works and land management, while the United States Army's Corps of Engineers spearheads the main stream reservoirs and levees or what is often referred to as the big dam interests.

People who live in large population areas within the flood hazards of a large river are interested in protection by reservoirs or levees. Oftentimes they want this protection regardless of the plight of agricultural interests situated on upstream tributaries.

Farmers who are well aware of tributary flood damage and soil erosion do not want to see major dam or downstream projects preclude them from flood protection. It is the contention of the tributary proponents that flood control at the source can reduce the necessity of constructing big dams for the protection of the downstream population areas. They realize that there must be a fusing of interests; that upstream projects are not the entire answer to the nation's annual floods.

In the years between 1936, when Congress first took cognizance of its responsibility in flood control by increasing the responsibility of the Corps of Engineers, and 1942, there was little conflict between the Department of Agriculture and the Corps of Engineers. This was because the Department of Agriculture was concerning itself almost exclusively with land management as a means of tributary control. Land management measures in addition to making strides in soil conservation and increased productivity proved valuable in flood control as well. The Department of Agriculture then started making recommendations for public works to reduce tributary flooding when it realized that land management alone could not alleviate agricultural damage due to upstream flooding. Construction of small upstream dams by the Department of Agriculture caused the

A victory for supporters of better Kansas flood control methods. Major General Lewis A. Pick, U. S. Corps of Engineers, addresses crowd at dedication of Kanopolis Dam. The $11,000,000 dam and reservoir, the first major project of the Pick-Sloan Plan, is a product of cooperation between the tributary control and the downstream advocates. At left of speaker is Senator Frank Carlson; on right, J. C. Mohler, Secretary of Agriculture, and A. Q. Miller, representing Kaw Valley Basin Flood Control Association. This was a big day for A. Q. Miller who has spent many years arguing the cause of a better overall flood control program for Kansas.

Corps of Engineers to assume a highly critical attitude and the controversy had begun.

There was justification for the concern of the engineers, just as there is justification for the Department of Agriculture's upstream flood control program. The Army pointed out that upstream flood control projects might make the construction of downstream dams seem unnecessary. These large dams are very expensive undertakings and the Army feared that appropriations would be reduced and the large dam program would fail. The Army further contended that the small upstream dams are incapable of containing a catastrophic flood and for this reason, the larger dam is still a necessity.

A. Q. Miller, who had been years ahead of his time in analyzing flood control methods, has foreseen this dissension. He has pointed out repeatedly that it is fallaceous to think that an upstream program can substitute for a downstream one or vice versa. Vociferous champions of one or the other programs often cause the public to become confused as to just what course the nation's flood control efforts should take. Actually the general public, up until a few years ago, has not been fully informed as to the merits of upstream or tributary flood control. Because A. Q. Miller has stumped editorially for recognition of the logic of upstream flood control projects does not mean that he advocates this method to the exclusion of all others.

"On the Kansas scene, from the time of the Kiro Dam proposal in 1933," says Miller, "I have espoused the cause of upstream or tributary control because I have been close to the problems of farmers and farm communities and I realized that any flood control program that sought only to contain flood waters downstream, after they had already reached dangerous proportions, was inadequate and inequitable. I have never been of the opinion that tributary control should be conducted at the expense of downstream projects and I have repeatedly striven for harmony between the two factions. Because of my role as spokesman in the fight for a tributary program, it has been assumed that this is my only interest. Such is not the case — I want to see a flood control program that is adequate in all respects and is the result of the combined thinking of the Department of Agriculture and the Corps of Engineers. Kansas' Kanopolis Dam is a shining example of such a combined project. It should be repeated throughout the nation."

CHAPTER VII

Government and Civic Activities

A Good Editor Is a Good Citizen

A. Q. MILLER'S publishing activities were marked by his constant participation in civic and government organizations. Interspersed with his journalistic work were several stints as an official of government.

As early as 1910 the late Arthur Capper, then Governor of Kansas, appointed A. Q. Miller Chairman of the State Board of Corrections. This service made a profound impression on Miller and he has preserved his recollections of this office in his papers.

Under supervision of the State Board of Corrections were the State Penitentiary at Lansing, the Reformatory at Hutchinson, the Boys Industrial School at Topeka, and the Girls Industrial School at Beloit. Once each month the Board met at the various institutions to consider cases of inmates eligible for parole.

Miller records in his memoirs: "For the first time I was convinced of the high percentage of delinquencies directly traceable to lack of home training and supervision. Many of the juvenile inmates' homes were nothing but 'coaling stations.'

There were actually cases of parents encouraging their children to commit minor crimes so that they could have the young offenders committed to an institution. The parents were thus freed of the responsibility of caring for their offspring.

"There was one case of a young boy who was confined in the Reformatory at Hutchinson, charged with burglary and larceny. What was this teenager's crime? The record showed that the youngster was so neglected at home that he actually did not get enough to eat. He pilfered food whenever he could. One day, while walking down an alley in Hutchinson, he smelled the cooking from an open restaurant window. He reached through the window and took a pie. Apprehended he was charged with 'burglary and larceny.' The lad's parents did not bother to appear at his trial and he was committed to the Reform School."

Miller notes in his papers that in many instances the parents of juvenile offenders should have been the ones tried for wrongs committed by their children.

Pressure in many forms was often brought to bear on the Board. A prominent citizen of Washington County had entered into a conspiracy with some crew members of a Burlington freight train. These men would jettison valuable freight at some isolated spot along the right of way and the Washington County citizen would pick it up. The ringleader soon found himself inside the bars. At previous parole board hearings at Lansing the relatives of the inmate appeared en masse "dressed in all their finery" and attempted to coerce favorable action from the board. When the new parole group met under the chairmanship of A. Q. Miller the Washington County inmate was brought before it again. The relatives were very much present and extremely miffed that their kin was not released. But the record was all the Board was interested in and it wasn't favorable to the freight pilferer.

It is interesting to note how the Parole Board functioned. The warden of the State Penitentiary at Lansing kept a complete dossier of all inmates (J. K. Codding was serving as warden when A. Q. Miller was on the State Board of Corrections). This dossier, in addition to containing all the information on the crime of which the inmate was accused, also had a profile of the attitude and general behaviour of the inmate. These records and the testimony of the warden, if desired, were the basis on which paroles were issued.

In his personal papers, A. Q. Miller comments that criminologists differ widely on how best to deal with a crime. Prevention before the criminal act is committed is the ideal, according to Miller. It pays off on the basic principle of dollars and cents. Local and state governments spend approximately five dollars to combat delinquency for every dollar spent on regular juvenile education. It costs as much to apprehend, convict and imprison a juvenile criminal as it does to send a boy through college, Miller notes.

The problem is still being fought with blackjacks, jail cells and reform schools, while the answer lies in prevention through education and understanding.

"My experience and observation has led me to the conclusion that there are thousands of criminals outside the penitentiaries who are never apprehended," remarks Miller. "Sometimes they have money and social position — this enables them to exercise political influence as well as avail themselves of the finest legal counsel.

"While many criminals remain free, the parolee who has paid his debt to society and wants to 'go straight' is often confronted with almost insurmountable obstacles. I saw an example of this myself while I was on the Board. At Lansing I had used the services of the prison barber shop and got to know one of the barbers quite well. He seemed a well adjusted young man and we granted him a parole as soon as he became eligible. Several years later I saw this same man in a Manhattan barber shop. I went in, waited until his chair was available, and got a shave. The paroled barber was having tough sledding. He had a wife and two children and was doing his utmost to lead a decent life. But several communities where he had worked had ostracized both him and his family when they learned of his prison record."

A. Q. Miller has remained keenly interested in penology and criminal rehabilitation as the result of his appointment to the Kansas State Board of Corrections back in 1910. Through his paper and participation in civic organizations, he has campaigned for progressive prisons where inmates might equip themselves for a normal life.

"There are criminal types who can never be rehabilitated, they are mentally maladjusted. But there are thousands who can become useful members of society if the society that placed them in prison enables them to improve their minds and then gives them a chance to prove themselves when they are released.

"No man should be obliged to serve a lifetime sentence of social ostracism for making one mistake," observes A. Q. Miller.

A. Q. Miller's next government appointment was in 1921. This came about in a rather unusual manner. Miller had placed a long distance telephone call from Belleville to Topeka. The operator gave him the wrong number and he found himself talking to H. H. Motter. This telephone conversation led to a meeting of the two men and later to Miller's appointment to the post of Division Chief, Salina Office, Bureau of Internal Revenue. Motter was Collector of Internal Revenue for the State of Kansas. This appointment actually changed the course of Miller's whole life. In order to accept the position Miller had to establish residence in Salina. This meant relinquishing the editorship of his beloved *Belleville Telescope.* However, since his son Carl had graduated from Kansas State a journalism major, he knew that he could leave the paper in competent hands. Then too, he would remain on the masthead as publisher and could continue to contribute editorials and features to the *Telescope.* Miller made his decision. Turning absolute control of the *Belleville Telescope* over to his son Carl, he moved to Salina and took up his new duties in the Department of Internal Revenue.

In the decade immediately following World War I income taxes did not pose the problem that they do now. A relatively small number of the population had incomes large enough to come under the provisions of the income tax law. At that time the major source of the Internal Revenue Department's activity was in connection with the enforcement of the Volstead Act.

H. H. Motter, in his capacity as Collector of Internal Revenue for the State of Kansas was notified to see that the Volstead Act was vigorously enforced. He notified George Wark, state prohibition enforcement director, to locate violators and file cases with the Collector of Internal Revenue in Wichita. Wark directed his enforcement campaign against distillers of "moonshine" for home consumption. In some cases, these operators also engaged in the sale of their product.

The Federal government kept an accurate record of all stills purchased. The owners were supposed to be using them for legal activities such as the distilling of water or for laboratory operation. Every purchaser of a still was to record the serial number with the Bureau of Internal Revenue and pay taxes on it. Field men from the Revenue Office periodically checked all purchasers of stills to make sure they had been properly registered and were not being used for illegal purposes.

When Wark ran into a series of Volstead Act violations in Ellis County, these individuals were hailed before the district court, paid a minimum fine and then went on about their business, thinking the matter had ended. They soon found out differently.

Mr. Wark had transcripts of the district court record made and turned these over to H. H. Motter. Motter, a conscientious government official, used these transcripts as the basis for assessing violations of the Volstead Act under Federal statutes. Here is what his assessments amounted to: Section 3265 R. S.—failure to register still $300; Section 222—25% penalty $125; Section 3265 R. S.—double tax violation $1,000; 25% penalty $250; interest at 6% $113.84: Total tax, penalty and interest came to $2,011.17.

The Ellis County violations became test cases under the new enforcement policy in Kansas. The Wichita office sent the cases, in the form of warrants, to the Division Office in Salina for collection. A. Q. Miller assigned E. D. Martin, deputy collector, the unenviable job of assembling the cases. The total amount involved was $11,544.16. Martin figured out the individual amounts due and presented the Bureau's demands. The delinquent parties, on the advice of their attorneys, refused to settle. Whereupon the Wichita office issued warrants to levy on any property, personal or real, in the possession of the offenders. Levies were made on the farms of the violators and, in accordance with instructions from the Bureau, notices were posted in three conspicuous places: on the property involved, in the Post Office, and in a local newspaper. Sale was fixed for 2:00 p.m., June 6, 1922.

One can well imagine the furor created by all of this. Public sympathy was very much with the individuals who sought to

The Republican State Central Committee for Kansas, 1920. (Left to right) — Walter Johnson, speakers bureau; H. H. Motter, chairman; A. Q. Miller, publicity director; Hugh Duff, treasurer, and George Beezley, secretary.

circumvent the law in order to assuage their thirst. The staff members in the office of the Bureau felt like genuine villains. But according to instructions Motter had received he had no alternative but to enforce the law to its very letter.

Of course the whole procedure was new and unprecedented and attracted widespread attention. The people and the legal profession were puzzled and metropolitan newspapers carried front page stories.

The violators were saved by a provision in the very same law that had placed them in such a predicament. There is a clause in the authority given the Collector of Internal Revenue called "Offer of Compromise." Under the provisions of this clause, the Collector, if he believes collection of a tax will work undue hardship on the taxpayer, may accept an offer in compromise if the taxpayer tenders such an offer. In the Ellis County test cases, attorneys for the violators advised them to go to the Wichita office before the date of the public sale of their farms and make an offer in compromise. This was done and all the cases were settled in the Wichita office.

As the result of these test cases, the Bureau of Internal Revenue received so much criticism that all pending cases were dropped. While everyone will agree that the penalties in the aforementioned test cases were too severe, especially for those individuals who were making liquor for their own use, this incident furnishes graphic evidence of the ineffectiveness of the Prohibition Amendment. While it was the law of the land, the general consensus of opinion was that it should not be enforced too rigorously or taken too seriously.

Not all the Bureau's efforts were directed toward dispossessing farmers from their land in order to satisfy tax claims. Working with H. H. Motter was a continual inspiration to Miller. Quin feels Motter was one of the most sincere and capable public servants he ever met. They became fast friends and Miller looks back on his tenure in the Salina office of the Bureau of Internal Revenue as a time well and happily spent.

In 1930, A. Q. Miller was named Executive Clerk of the United States Senate by Senator Henry J. Allen of Kansas. Miller's duties in the nation's capitol gave him ample opportunity to observe the political scene first hand. He considered this appointment by Senator Allen as one of the highlights of his career of political service.

Strangely enough while Miller has always been a staunch and outspoken Republican and an inveterate "standpat conservative," his most responsible political appointment was received from President Franklin D. Roosevelt. On the morning of January 24, 1934, he received the following telegram from the White House:

> "I have today appointed you member of advisory committee of three for your state under the Public Works Administration. I hope you can accept.
>
> Franklin D. Roosevelt"

Two days later Miller received a two-page letter from the President outlining some of the duties of the board to which he had been appointed.

The Public Works Program was a measure enacted by Congress as a means of alleviating the nation's unemployment problem. At this time there were some 13,000,000 Americans without jobs. Projects provided for by the PWA were such public construction as roads, bridges, court houses, municipal buildings, etc. As a matter of fact, Belleville's very beautiful court house is an example of some of the fine and useful work done by the PWA.

A. Q. Miller's work on the board with the two Democratic members proved to be a rich experience and was one of his finest associations in public life. At the very first meeting Miller made a gesture to Arthur L. Mellott, chairman, that the majority mem-

Lynn R. Broderick, left, prominent Kansas Democratic figure, and lifelong friend of A. Q. Miller, congratulates A. Q. on the latter's receipt of his fifty-year Masonic pin. Broderick and Miller have been friends since they shared hotel accommodations at early meetings of the Kansas State Editorial Association. They have remained close friends over a lifetime despite their different political loyalties.

bers would probably decide on the projects to be approved. Mellott promptly and emphatically disclaimed the assertion by requesting full and open participation in all board matters. He further emphasized that all board problems would be considered on top of the table. This is exactly the way in which the business of the board was conducted.

Federal Judge Arthur J. Mellott, formerly an attorney for one of the government's important war boards, is an extremely fine example of political integrity and devotion to his country's welfare, according to A. Q. Miller.

Obviously the service of the board was considered largely an engineering function. Very shortly after the initial meeting, all boards in the region were called to Little Rock, Arkansas. Here they were practically liquidated. All work was turned over to state engineers to check on economic soundness of the various projects.

Following the abolishment of the state PWA boards, Miller was placed on the executive board of the state's public works program because of his familiarity and experience with flood control and soil conservation problems. Evan Griffith was state director of the program. At the time of Miller's appointment, the principal work projects consisted of building farm ponds with Federal Aid. Standard specifications were given through the office of George Knapp, state engineer of water resources. As a result of this program, thousands of farm ponds were built all over the state. These not only served as stock ponds but brought up the water table, retarded water run off and aided in the very important problem of soil conservation.

During the middle years of the depression, many thousands of "white collar" workers were among the unemployed. Their talents could not be utilized to fullest advantage on construction projects. The Federal government proposed the compilation of a series of State Guide Books, to form ultimately the *American*

Guide, as a project that would be useful and also give employment to many types of white collar workers.

At the time this project was being organized a representative from Washington contacted state director Evan Griffith to obtain a suitable director for the Kansas project. When the Washington official made known that he wanted an experienced newspaperman for this post, Griffith recommended A. Q. Miller and he was summoned to Topeka for a conference.

The Washington representative presented the project to Miller in glowing terms. The guide books were to contain historical facts and geographical data concerning each and every state. The project was to be a useful one. Miller agreed to take on the task of editing the Kansas work. He was to organize the state by counties, hire white collar workers with writing ability, preferably any newspapermen who were on the unemployment rolls. It seemed that this project was indeed a useful one. Miller, who had always been interested in history, especially where it pertained to Kansas, was enthusiastic about the new undertaking. More so than ever when he was assured by the Washington official that the task was to be completely devoid of politics and he would have a free hand in handling the Kansas phase of the *American Guide.*

Miller opened an office in Topeka and began the new work with keen interest. He visited many sections of the state and used all means at his disposal to publicize the project and locate qualified people for the writing jobs. He was extremely fortunate in being able to man the state office with highly qualified and experienced writers. Under Miller's supervision, a happy and loyal organization was formed. Some of his enthusiasm for the project seemed to infect every member of the staff.

In other parts of the state work was also progressing smoothly. Research was being carried on at the county level and much hitherto unpublished history was being uncovered. The Kansas

Guide Book project had an excellent rating in Washington and Miller and his co-workers were pleased with what they had accomplished thus far. Suddenly another Washington representative made an unannounced visit to Topeka, ostensibly to check on the progress of the Kansas project. This individual proceeded to disrupt the organization Miller had worked so patiently to build. His literary taste was confined to the sensational. All he had previously heard or read about Kansas had to do with cyclones, dust storms and heat waves, and he wanted these phenomena duly recorded in the Kansas Guide Book.

Miller demurred, protesting that such incidents were not a typical or true picture of the Kansas scene. A. Q. pointed out to the new arrival that Kansas had a fine educational, cultural and civic tradition and that it was one of the nation's outstanding agricultural states. It was also shaping up as far as its industrial development. Despite Miller's protestations the Washington delegate insisted that a full chapter of the Kansas Guide Book be devoted to the "Dust Bowl."

Very patiently A. Q. pointed out that the infamous "Dust Bowl" was not a product of Kansas. It was a product of the plains regions in the Southwest, comprised of the Texas Panhandle, the western third of Oklahoma, southeastern Colorado, the western third of Nebraska and the western third of Kansas. So why, reasoned Miller, should Kansas be held responsible for this trick of nature. Nevertheless the man from Washington insisted that Miller's staff of writers should follow his suggestions in writing the history of Kansas.

Finally, the official departed and Miller was able to restore order in the wake of the chaos he created. Next an order was issued from the National Director of the American Guide in Washington requesting that a complete "dummy" of the Kansas project be completed. This was to be departmentalized and have a suggested cover page. Thirty days were given for completion of the assignment. Miller's staff was jubilant. Here was a chance to show Washington what they could do. Pouring over the huge files which had been accumulated, the staff worked enthusiastically, even putting in their nights on a voluntary basis so the deadline could be met.

After the "dummy" had been sent, Miller inquired as to its disposition. He received no reply. Finally, after writing Washington repeatedly, he received a letter from the national director advising him that all plans had been changed in regard to the type of copy and general character of the *American Guide* series. New specifications were supposed to be in the mail and Miller was advised to destroy all the copy previously prepared. One can easily imagine the disappointment and disillusionment of Miller's staff. Months of field and office work were a total loss and morale sank to a visible low.

Several weeks passed with no new instructions forthcoming from Washington. Finally another letter was received announcing that all state directors were to meet the national chief in Salt Lake City for an important conference. Upon arriving in Salt Lake City, Miller found that the chief was in California and had sent a substitute to conduct the conference. A day later the chief arrived in Salt Lake. The first day's session had proven fruitless, no new plan had been suggested. When the national director arrived, an important meeting was called for Thursday at 10:00 a.m.

All the state directors were in their places when the hour rolled around but no one appeared to preside over the meeting. Finally word was received that the national director had been called back to Washington. He had left no official instructions with the state directors and they were compelled to return to their various organizations without any new information of any kind. The entire undertaking was at a standstill.

SALINA CHAMBER OF COMMERCE - - - SALINA, KANSAS

AWARD
FOR DISTINGUISHED SERVICE

BE IT KNOWN THAT THE BOARD OF DIRECTORS AND THE MEMBERS OF THE HIGHWAY COMMITTEE HEREBY RECOGNIZE

A. Q. MILLER

FOR THIRTY-SIX YEARS OF OUTSTANDING SERVICE TO THIS COMMUNITY IN THE ORGANIZATION AND ESTABLISHMENT OF U. S. 81 PAN-AMERICAN HIGHWAY

BOARD OF DIRECTORS

PRESIDENT

1ST VICE-PRES.

2ND VICE-PRES.

MGR.-SEC.

HIGHWAY COMMITTEE

CHAIRMAN

Distinguished service award presented A. Q. Miller by a grateful community in appreciation of his years of effort toward civic betterment.

A. Q. Miller was so disheartened by this fiasco that he submitted his resignation to Washington as soon as he reached home.

"I felt very badly about this situation," said Miller, "I had looked forward so keenly to completing the Kansas project and can honestly say that my entire staff worked devotedly toward this objective. When the objective was changed, or I should say eliminated, and we were given no alternate plan, I couldn't see what purpose I was serving and thereupon resigned.

"I realize that the administration was trying to do a big job at this time and that many incidents were unavoidable. However, a good deal of the confusion was the result of a top heavy bureaucracy which, in my opinion, seemed to be the hall mark of this administration."

A. Q. Miller's tenure of service during the Roosevelt administration was his last official participation as a government appointee.

"I am grateful for the opportunities I had to serve in government," reports Miller. "I learned much from my various services and formed many friendships which I shall always cherish. Despite my personal criticism of a few individuals and a few incidents, I have been favorably impressed with the quality and devotion of the men in government, both Democrat and Republican, with whom I have been privileged to work."

An indefatigable worker for the Republican party, A. Q. Miller has been repeatedly cited by that organization. He has served tirelessly on both county, state and national publicity boards and campaigned actively for Kansas candidates. His *Belleville Telescope* printing plant has turned out tons of campaign literature on a cost basis. This despite the fact that political printing is generally looked upon as quite a financial plum.

In recognition of the major contributions A. Q. Miller has made to the journalism profession of Kansas he was elected president of the Kansas State Editorial Association in 1940 and continues to serve this organization in an advisory capacity.

During the war years, A. Q. Miller headed up the War Bond drive in Salina County and through his effort put this county over its quota consistently.

The Salina Chamber of Commerce recently presented its former president, A. Q. Miller, with a distinguished service award acknowledging his thirty-six years of outstanding service to his community and the state of Kansas and his part in the organization of U. S. 81 — Pan American Highway.

In 1949, seven Kansas counties combined in an effort to obtain his appointment to the Board of Directors of the United States Chamber of Commerce to represent Agriculture. In the vigorous campaign for Miller's appointment, his qualifications were presented thusly:

"A. Q. Miller is a newspaper man and an acknowledged authority on Agriculture. Never a farmer himself, but as a successful newspaper publisher serving predominantly an agricultural area, Mr. Miller has taken a keen interest in Agriculture — its problems and their ramifications. Kansas known principally as a wheat farming state is, as a matter of fact, highly diversified in its farming activities. Corn, oats, barley, sorghums, soybeans, sugar beets... even cotton and flax are but a few of its farm products. Poultry, dairy farming, hogs, sheep and beef cattle are all major farm industries.

"Mr. Miller is qualified to represent Agriculture on the Board of the Chamber of Commerce of the United States. He knows the subject of Agriculture and all its ramifications intimately... marketing... transportation... and processing. All this, not merely as regards the midwest and its crop alone, but over the nation as a whole, for he has traveled widely throughout the United States and has been a keen observer and interested student wherever he has gone."

This summation of Miller's interest in agriculture could very aptly be applied to all those subjects in which he is keenly interested. He learns the overall national scene and then applies it to the Kansas scene. Because of this his outlook has always been a broad one, though looking at the world through Kansas glasses he is well aware of the problems of Kansas in relation to the nation as a whole.

A. Q. Miller has served his community and his state wherever possible. He never asked how much was required of him or how much it was going to cost. He asked only if he could help get the job done. During his sixty some years as a Kansas publisher and public servant he has helped get a good many jobs done. He will always be remembered for his community spirit and good citizenship, attributes which sometime seem to be fading from the American scene.

CHAPTER VIII

The "Journalistic" Millers

A Newspaper Family

ON A HOT midsummer day, July 17, 1896, Lloyd Rayburn Miller, first son of Quin and Martha Miller, was born. Lloyd first saw the light of day in a frame house that Clifton's young editor was renting for six dollars a month. With the birth of their first child, Quin and Martha began planning for his future as well as the future of any brothers and sisters.

Lloyd's parents were determined that the newest member of the Miller family should have every opportunity that they could possibly give him. At the same time they realized that a child must learn to stand on his own feet. Neither Lloyd nor his four brothers and one sister had things handed to them on a silver platter. From the birth of their first son, the Miller family was a working partnership. Quin worked all the harder to develop the *Clifton News* and Martha managed the household and the new baby with efficiency.

Lloyd was exposed early to the newspaper business. When he was old enough to attend elementary school, the family had located in Belleville, Kansas, and Lloyd began putting in an appearance at the office of the *Belleville Telescope* on his way

An early picture of the entire Miller family. Top row: Luman G., A. Q., Jr., Lloyd, Carl P. and Merle. Bottom row: Enola, A. Q., Sr., and Martha Patterson Miller. This photograph was taken in 1931.

home from school. Fascinated by the mechanical phases of the printing business, Lloyd could nearly always be found in the back room performing whatever chores might be delegated him. He was waiting for a chance to operate some of the machinery which printed the *Telescope.* By the time he was graduated from high school, Lloyd was an extremely proficient Linotype operator.

Quin Miller takes no credit for the fact that all of his children finished college. According to their Dad, all of the children actually earned their keep after they got out of the knee pants stage.

It is significant that Quin Miller took pains to insure that "newspapering" was not forced upon the children. Each of the young Millers gravitated to the family publishing enterprise like young ducks to water. They seemed to have it in their blood and once they got printers' ink under their fingernails, they never lost their interest.

Lloyd attended Kansas State College, Manhattan, Kansas. He was a member of the Sigma Nu fraternity and active in campus affairs. He was graduated in 1920 with a Bachelor of Science degree in Civil Engineering. For Lloyd Miller, the primary fascination of the family newspaper had been in the mechanical department. This experience was responsible for his selection of civil engineering as a profession rather than journalism.

Lloyd's college career was interrupted by a stint in the Navy during World War I. Upon his return he graduated from Kansas State College and worked at engineering in many capacities in several Kansas localities. In 1923 he was with the State Highway Commission in Topeka. As a registered professional civil engineer, Lloyd was resident engineer on many Federal highway projects. In this capacity, Lloyd was participating in the construction of good roads, a subject about which he heard so much from his father as a youngster. During World War II, he worked as a civilian for the U. S. Army Engineers in the District Office at Albuquerque, New Mexico.

During his interesting career as an engineer, Lloyd still retained a keen interest in the newspaper business. In 1943, he returned to newspaper work in Colorado. In 1947, he went to Covina, California, to work with his brothers, Carl P. and A. Q. Jr., who needed his services in their expanding newspaper enterprise.

Lloyd was married to Elda J. Johnson, a childhood sweetheart, at Belleville, Kansas, on August 10, 1918. They have two children, a daughter, Mrs. Anna Marie Ball of Casper, Wyoming, a son, Dr. M. L. Miller of Sterling, Colorado; and five grandchildren.

Carl Patterson Miller, the second child of A. Q. and Martha, was born October 30, 1897. It was the prospect of Carl on the scene that decided Quin on the desirability of seeking a more lucrative publishing enterprise. Shortly before Carl's birth, Quin bought the *Riley Regent* in Riley, Kansas. The Riley paper had a greater potential than the *Clifton News,* and Quin Miller believed that he could develop the paper and with it provide better for his increasing family responsibilities.

Carl got his first test of the "glamour" of newspaper work when he and his older brother, Lloyd, accompanied their father on his jaunts to the county seat and other nearby towns. Combining business with pleasure, Quin would hitch up Prince to his one-seated buggy, and with two stools in front of the dashboard for his two young sons, he would tour about the county. Lloyd still says that his prominent ears are a result of the flapping of the reins across his ears, and both of the boys still recall the switching of the horse's tail in their faces.

For Carl the newspaper was a continuing source of interest.

When A. Q. Miller, Sr., visited his son Carl, in California, three generations of Rotarians were represented at the Covina Rotary Club; Carl P. Miller, Jr., A. Q. Miller, Sr., and Carl P. Sr. Carl, Sr., is a past president of the Rotary Club of Los Angeles and past district governor of Rotary International.

He never got over this fascination and, like his father, he decided early upon a journalistic career. Carl, like Lloyd, started working in the *Belleville Telescope* office while still a youngster. He performed all of the routine chores assigned to Quin Miller's young "printer's devils" and enjoyed every one of them, with the possible exception of sweeping out the shop. He learned to set type at an early age and, to enable him to reach the "upper case," his father placed him on top of an American Type Founders' catalogue atop a high stool.

While attending Kansas State College, where he majored in journalism, Carl, during his junior year, was business manager of the Kansas State Collegian, the college daily. Milton Eisenhower, Ike's brother, was a member of the staff. Carl was the campus correspondent of the Associated Press, *Kansas City Star* and *Times, Omaha World-Herald, St. Louis Post-Dispatch,* and *Topeka Daily Capital.* During his other years at Kansas State, he was city editor of the *Manhattan Daily Mercury* (published by Fay N. Seaton) and the *Manhattan Nationalist* (published by Ed Shellenbaum). At Kansas State, Carl was a member of Sigma Delta Chi, national professional journalist fraternity, and Sigma Nu, social fraternity.

Immediately after leaving Kansas State, Carl took over the management and editorial responsibilities of the *Belleville Telescope.* This enabled Quin Miller to accept the appointment as Division Chief of the Internal Revenue Service at Salina. While he remained the publisher, Quin Miller turned over all the reins of management to his son, Carl. Carl married Marvel Merillat, a college sweetheart, on September 24, 1920. Early in 1925 Carl Miller heard about Longview, Washington, an ideal town being conceived and built by R. A. Long of Kansas City, a millionaire lumber dealer. The glowing descriptions of the growing community captured Carl's fancy. Turning the management of the *Belleville Telescope* over to his sister, Enola, Carl, with his wife and 13-month old son, Carl, Jr., headed west in his three-door Willys-Knight car.

Sightseeing, en route to Longview, Carl and his family decided to spend a week in Southern California. He fell so much in love with Los Angeles that he decided to see if he could locate there instead of Longview. He gathered up his credentials and made a call at the *Los Angeles Times* to see what the job picture was. The following Monday he went to work in the Financial Editorial Department of the *Los Angeles Times.* He later became Assistant Financial Editor. The *Los Angeles Times,* even in the twenties, was one of the largest and most influential newspapers in the United States. It was a mighty leap from editor of the *Belleville Telescope* to the staff of such a journalistic giant. Carl took it all in stride. Realizing that fundamentals were fundamentals, regardless of the scope of the operation, he applied what he learned in journalism school and on the home town paper to his work with the *Times.* He left the *Times* to become Manager of the New York News Bureau in 1927, and in 1928 became associated with the Los Angeles Stock Exchange as Assistant Manager and later became Secretary and Manager. In 1929, when the *Wall Street Journal* was preparing to establish its Pacific Coast Edition, Carl Miller was asked by Kenneth C. Hogate, then editor and publisher of the *Journal,* to head up the Pacific Coast publication. Eager to get back into journalism, Carl associated himself with the *Wall Street Journal* in 1929 and has directed the Pacific Coast activities since.

Always a believer in the importance of service organizations, Carl early became active in the affairs of Rotary International and the Los Angeles Chamber of Commerce. He had organized the Lions Club in Belleville, Kansas, in 1923. In 1939 he was president of the Los Angeles Rotary Club and in 1951-52 he was Governor of District 160 of Rotary International. He was a member of the Magazine Committee of Rotary International for three years and was Chairman in 1954-55. He has been Treasurer of the Los Angeles Rotary Club for the past five years. Carl has been a member of the Board of Directors of the Los Angeles Chamber of Commerce for eight years, was Chairman of its Research Committee for six years, was Vice-President in 1954 and President in 1955. This honor by the world's greatest Chamber of Commerce is official recognition of his untiring efforts in behalf of his adopted city.

Carl and his wife, Ruth, (Carl's first wife, Marvel, passed away in October, 1948, and Carl married Ruth Bohe in July, 1950) reside in Covina, a few freeway minutes from his office at the *Wall Street Journal* in downtown Los Angeles. As the area where he lived started to grow in the middle forties, Carl founded San Gabriel Valley Newspapers, Inc., and, with his brother, A. Q., Jr., and other newspaper friends, developed a newspaper chain to serve the growing area. The chain now includes the *San Gabriel Valley Daily Tribune* and four weekly papers, all in the area of the East San Gabriel Valley where Carl lives.

Carl's son, Carl, Jr., married Betty Reed of Covina in 1948, and is engaged in the land development business in the Covina area; and his daughter, Martha Irene, was married in August, 1955, to William Kerckhoff, son of a pioneer California family.

Kansas is as proud of Carl Miller as Californa. Carl attributes his accomplishments to his Kansas heritage and the sound lessons in good citizenship and journalistic ethics he learned from his parents.

Quin and Martha's only daughter, Enola, was born June 18, 1899, at Riley, Kansas. From the very start, Enola was determined that being a girl was not going to bar her from the fascinating domain of the *Telescope.* Despite the taunts of her two brothers, Enola took up her duties in the front office.

Lloyd and Carl soon had to concede that Enola was good for something else besides playing with dolls. Moreover, her presence in the shop freed them for more advanced duties. Enola entered Kansas State in 1918, majoring in journalism and interior decorating. Enola had moved, with her parents, to Salina when the editorial chores of the *Telescope* had been turned over to Carl. After graduating from Kansas State, she had a gift shop in Salina until 1924. On June 29, 1924, Enola was married to William Clark Perry.

When Carl left for the Pacific Coast in 1925, A. Q., Jr., was still in college and Enola took over as editor of the *Telescope.* During her high school and early college days she had handled society as well as reportorial assignments on the *Telescope* and was well qualified to supervise the family publication. In the spring of 1926, A. Q., Jr., fresh from Kansas State, relieved Enola as editor of the *Telescope.* Enola had a more important assignment. Her son, William Clark Perry, Jr., was born on March 13, 1926. A daughter, Jo Anne Kay, was born on April 22, 1930.

In 1937, Enola and her husband moved to Pendleton, Oregon, where W. C. Perry was associated in law practice with Charles Z. Randall. A very able and successful trial lawyer, Bill Perry was appointed Circuit Judge at Pendleton, Oregon, in 1950. He was elevated to the Supreme Court of the State of Oregon in December of 1952.

In June of 1944 the Perrys' young daughter, Jo Anne, met a very untimely death. In the same month, Bill, Jr., entered the Navy. With her family disrupted, Enola found solace in work. She returned to her newspaper career as a staff writer for the *Pendleton East Oregonian.* She remained there for two years handling society and feature stories.

When the *East Oregonian* was preparing material for its 75th Anniversary Edition in 1946, they sought Enola Perry's services. As a full time society reporter she assisted them in the compilation of their anniversary edition.

The Perrys' son, Bill, Jr., attended Oregon University and Eastern Oregon College of Education. He served in the Navy from 1944 until 1946. On June 29, 1949, his parents' twenty-fifth wedding anniversary, he was married to Janet Eaton of Pendleton. The young Perrys have two children, Jo Anne Kay, named for Bill, Jr.'s sister, and William Clark Perry, III.

Enola Miller Perry has played an active part in the affairs of communities in which she has lived. During the hectic years of World War II she served on ration boards, hospital auxiliary groups and many other organizations where the only reward for one's service is the satisfaction of knowing that a useful job is being done. At the present time, Enola Perry is chairman of all Volunteer Service Groups for the Marion County Red Cross.

Enola has always been grateful for her interest and education in journalism.

A. Q. Miller, Jr., who succeeded Enola as editor of the *Belleville Telescope,* was born on July 13, 1905, at Belleville, Kansas. Young A. Q., Jr., also majored in journalism at Kansas State College. During the summer vacations he worked on the *Salina Daily Union.*

In the spring of 1926, A. Q., Jr., took over the editorship of the *Telescope.* On August 6, 1926, he was married to Ulene Leedom of Belleville. He continued as editor of the *Telescope* until the spring of 1936. Under A. Q., Jr.'s management, the *Telescope* made great progress, became Kansas' greatest weekly, and won many national and state journalism awards for excellence and merit. A. Q., Jr., was a member of Casey's All-American Newspaper Eleven in 1933. He won the N. E. A. circulation progress contest in 1932 and many other awards. In 1936, he moved to Ontario, California, to become advertising manager of the *Ontario Daily Report.* One year later he became general manager of the *Daily Report* and served in that capacity for ten years.

A. Q., Jr., then purchased the *Ontario Herald,* a weekly. He operated this newspaper for a year before selling out to become associated with his brother Carl in the publishing venture in Covina, California. He assisted Carl in the formation of their corporation, known as *San Gabriel Valley Newspapers, Inc.* A. Q., Jr., now serves this ever growing enterprise as executive vice president and treasurer, and is active in civic and community affairs.

A. Q., Jr., and his wife, Ulene, make their home in Covina, California. They have three daughters: Marilyn, now Mrs. Ernest Pellkofer; Alexandra Q., a student at the University of California at Los Angeles, and Judith, a grammar school student. The Pellkofers have two sons, Ernest III and Stephen.

When A. Q., Jr., left for California, his younger brothers, Merle and Luman, assumed the management of the *Belleville Telescope.* Merle Monroe Miller was born April 21, 1915, in Belleville, Kansas. He was reared, however, in Salina, Kansas. In 1932 he enrolled at Kansas State College as a journalism major.

Merle was married to Erma Ann Schmedemann of Manhattan, Kansas, on September 4, 1938.

Merle was assisted in his management of the *Telescope* by his younger brother Luman Miller. The two brothers divided the supervisory duties of the paper, with Merle functioning as advertising and business manager and Luman as editor.

While Luman was in the Navy, Merle operated the paper practically single handed. In June, 1955, Merle purchased his

The Millers, a Sigma Delta Chi family. When Merle, A. Q.'s fourth son, became a member of Sigma Delta Chi, national journalism fraternity, the other Sigma Delta Chi's in the family gathered for this photograph. Top row: Carl P. Miller, past national president of Sigma Delta Chi, and A. Q. Miller, Jr. Bottom row: Luman G. Miller, A. Q., Sr., and Merle Miller.

brother's interest in the *Telescope* and now publishes the paper in a partnership with his father.

The Merle Millers have three children: Monte, Mark and a daughter, Margo. Merle is active in civic as well as publishing circles having served as a board member of the Belleville Chamber of Commerce and an official in the Boy Scouts of America. He has been instrumental in developing the North Central Kansas Free Fair into one of Kansas' outstanding community affairs. He is also active in Kansas press circles.

Luman G. Miller, the youngest of the Miller family, worked closely with his brother Merle, in the operation of the *Belleville Telescope.* Born July 10, 1916, Luman is fifteen months younger than Merle and the two brothers served their early apprenticeship on the family newspaper together. From 1938 until 1955, Luman was editor of the paper. This interval was interrupted by service in the Navy during World War II. Luman was a Naval Public Information Officer and was separated from the service as Lieutenant (j.g.).

He attended the University of California at Los Angeles and received his journalism degree from Kansas State College. A past president of the Belleville Chamber of Commerce and the Belleville Lions Club, Luman was also a trustee of the William Allen White Foundation of the University of Kansas, Lawrence.

In June of 1955, Luman became editor and publisher of *The Dalles Daily Chronicle,* The Dalles, Oregon. He and his wife, the former Jane Phelan of Kansas City, Missouri, and their four children: Patricia Ann, Catherine, Jimmy and Tommy, now make their home in The Dalles.

For many years at gatherings of the Kansas press, the following question was heard: "Well, I wonder which of the young Miller clan is editing A. Q.'s *Telescope* now?" Despite accusations that he planned his family so that his newspaper would have an assured source of talent, A. Q., Sr., maintains that it just happened to work out that way.

Quin Miller has always insisted that the only credit he can take for his very fine family is the fact that he had enough sense to choose their mother. Those who know Martha Patterson Miller are free to admit that Quin is partly right. Martha Miller reared her family firmly and justly. She was never too busy to lend them sympathy and encouragement when it was needed.

All of the Miller children look back on their childhood as a wonderfully happy and useful time. Under the guidance of their mother they learned to share the chores, the good fortune and the bad times. Each of the children received a thorough grounding in Christian principles. What is more important, they saw the principles they were taught being lived. There is no finer instruction than example. Martha and A. Q. Miller practiced what they preached.

In 1941, Mrs. A. Q. Miller was selected regional American Mother of Kansas by the American Mothers' Committee of the Golden Rule Foundation. The title of Regional Mother was bestowed on Mrs. Miller as "representative of the best there is in motherhood."

Kansas newspapers in reporting the singular honors accorded Mrs. Miller had this to say:

"Martha P. Miller may well be called the 'press muse' for her husband as well as her children are vitally concerned with journalism. Born in Clifton, Clay County, Kansas, she was reared in a Scotch Presbyterian home. Her mother died when she was 15 years old and she assumed the household duties while completing her high school education. She was valedictorian of her graduating class.

"She married A. Q. Miller, a young country newspaper publisher, and reared a large and successful family. As the mother of six children, it was necessary for Martha Miller to do all of her own work until the children were large enough to help. She did all the family sewing and besides her household duties found time to assist and encourage her children with their studies. As soon as the children were old enough, they were taught to work and assume responsibility. From the time they were tall enough to reach the typesetting cases they worked on the family newspaper.

"Mrs. Miller still found time to take an active part in community affairs. She has always been active in the work of the Presbyterian Church and various church auxiliaries. She was a member of the P.E.O., the Belleville and Salina Parent-Teacher Association, the Twentieth Century and the Federation of Womens Clubs.

"Endowed with a sound sense of Scotch thrift, Martha Miller managed her large family well on what was often a meager income. Each of the six Miller children received a college education which in itself was a major accomplishment."

On October 9, 1955, the entire clan of "journalistic Millers" will honor A. Q. and Martha Miller on their sixtieth wedding anniversary. The five sons and one daughter, together with granddaughters and grandsons, are converging on the family home in Salina for this great event.

A. Q. and Martha Miller, a Kansas couple who started with a small country weekly, their love for one another, and a pocketful of dreams, are extremely proud of their fine family. Their dreams were not for great wealth or prestige, just the sincere hope that they might rear their children wisely and well so that these children would be a credit to their God, their country and their community. A. Q. and Martha Miller have realized their dreams, their children are the proof.

CHAPTER IX

Outstanding Editorials

WHY THE *Belleville Telescope* IS ONE OF THE NATION'S BEST

NEXT to publishing the news of the day, the most important contribution of any newspaper is that of influencing and molding public opinion through its editorial columns. The news columns must present the news in a factual and completely unbiased manner. There is no room for the expression of opinions in a news story. The editorial columns, however, permit the editor to express his own opinions and make pertinent comment on the news that his paper carries. From these opinions readers draw their own conclusions; they may agree or disagree with those of the editor. No newspaper lacking an aggressive editorial policy will achieve any measure of fame. This is particularly true of the country weekly.

A. Q. Miller's editorials in the *Belleville Telescope* are read avidly by the people of Republic county and a great number of distinguished citizens outside the county. Readers may not always agree with Miller but they know his sage comments are the result of a lifetime as an observer of the local and national scene.

A cross section of A. Q. Miller's editorial efforts has been selected from the files of the *Belleville Telescope.* These deal with a variety of events and subjects from a tribute to a fellow Republican, Herbert Hoover, to a *Soldier's Right to Vote.*

Examination of these editorials will show what a great fund of information A. Q. Miller has acquired on national and international affairs and how he bases his editorial conclusions on this knowledge. His editorials have won many awards for the *Belleville Telescope.* The fact that his fellow newsmen rate his observations so highly is a great tribute to his journalistic ability.

RESTORE CONFIDENCE IN GOVERNMENT

Last week the Government faced one of the greatest domestic crises in its history — it faced the threat of a complete breakdown in authority over 140,000,000 people; it faced the decision of whether or not any individual or any group could defy constitutional authority under our American system.

The crisis called for courageous and vigorous action on the part of constituted government authority. President Truman, who still retains his war powers, arose to the occasion and challenged the right of anyone to strike against the Government, as he called it. Government machinery set up to settle labor disputes failed to function and it remained for the Government either to step in and use its constitutional powers or witness a complete paralysis of the economic life of the country. The President called Congress into joint session and requested unprecedented authority to deal with the problem. He told Congress: "The rail strike is no longer a dispute between labor and management — it has now become a strike against the Government itself. That kind of strike," said the President, "can never be tolerated in this country; if allowed to continue, government itself will break down; strikes against the government must stop, therefore I request immediate legislation designed to help stop them." These were strong words and brave words, though issued somewhat belatedly. Congress cheered the President lustily and White House aides reported that an avalanche of telegrams and letters poured into the White House such as had never before been experienced during the Truman administration.

One writer on national affairs said: "Radical labor leaders, smug in their gain of 12 years under the New Deal, had become arrogant and were not afraid to challenge a government which had always been sympathetic toward their aims." A blight had settled down upon the country and an epidemic of strikes had halted production so much needed to stop inflation in the reconversion program.

John D. Small, Civilian Production Administrator, said: "The coal strike alone has cost the country $2,000,000,000 in lost production, not counting the loss in wages of millions of dollars." In Chicago a 9-day dim-out on account of the coal strike cost $131,000,000, and in Detroit the Ford Motor Co. lost $500,000,000 in production besides a loss in wages of Ford employees of $237,000,000. These are samples of how the economic system of the country was being paralyzed and the Government seemed impotent to act effectively.

It is not a happy thought to say that people were becoming disillusioned and expressions of lack of faith in the Government were being heard across the country, and it was not a happy picture in this stronghold of democracy for foreign countries to see. It is imperative for Congress to act to preserve constitutional government under our American system, and if the President does not have the authority under his emergency powers, Congress should give him sufficient authority to compose labor-management difficulties and set up machinery for the equitable adjudication of labor-management disputes.

June 6, 1946

"PRIMROSE PATH" AND NATIONAL SECURITY

It must be obvious to the casual observer, who has any concern about the future of his country, that if it does not change its course, America is marching down the "primrose path" to national bankruptcy and the possibility of atomic war — unless the people awaken from their indifference, complacency and lethargy and see that public officials are elected to office who think more of the welfare of their country than they do of their political party.

In recent elections — local, state and national — an average of 40 percent of the qualified voters have not gone to the polls and voted. This means that the nation is governed by 60 per cent of the electorate, which is composed largely of politicians, would-be politicians, candidates who make the biggest compromises, and voters receiving government checks and subsidies. In the present trend there are plenty of danger signals along the road for those who will stop, look and listen and direct their thinking above personal, mercenary and selfish gains, and give some thought to the welfare of their children and future generations.

Read the following from the *Bloomington* (Ill.) *Pantagraph,* whose editor sounds a warning and danger signal to its readers:

"A little Bloomington girl of 11 was reading the paper at breakfast. She ran across this paragraph: 'President Truman said that he alone will decide whether this country will try to produce the hydrogen bomb, and that he has no idea when the decision will be made.'

"The 11-year-old said: 'Daddy, I thought Congress decided things like that'."

So did a lot of other American citizens until the President and his appointees began to assume a military dictatorship in this country. Now Congress has little to do about it. Congress lets the President fire the chief of naval operations because he said some things before a congressional committee that displeased the President. The fact that Mr. Truman, his Secretary of Defense, his Secretary of the Navy and the congressional committee promised the Navy chief that there would be no reprisals did not matter.

Congress is at fault because Congress should correct the situation. Congress hasn't done so because, as Edgar Ansel Mowrer pointed out, the "wise men on Capitol Hill are as eager as many American citizens to get a cheap, easy victory by hot air power."

If Mr. Truman can build the new H-bomb to guarantee us "security without tears," Congress appears to be willing. Quoting Mr. Mowrer again: "We'll just go ahead and build a new bomb a thousand times more destructive than those which split open Hiroshima and Nagasaki. Then having re-established our monopoly on the latest absolute weapon, we can go back to normal interests — bigger profits, wage increases, more free services and pensions and insurance, with public interest centered on matters like the Boston robbery and Hollywood love life."

So we leave our defense to the propaganda boys in the Air Force who assure us that all we need to do is give them plenty of B-36 bombers and the latest "absolute weapon" and we may sleep in safety. We leave the decisions to Mr. Truman and his politically appointed henchmen who run the military show. We go right on believing in a cheap, easy victory without bloodshed or toil.

And we are likely to find that we lack the sea power to take overseas bases, transport troops and supplies and free the seas of enemy submarines. We are almost certain to find that we are more subject to the A-bombs and the H-bombs than will be our enemies.

We don't seem to recall that the A-bomb security lasted a very short time. We don't appear willing to understand that bombs never did win a war and are not likely to win one in the foreseeable future. It takes ground forces and naval forces. Yet we are letting Mr. Truman and his henchmen starve our Army and our Navy without protest.

Yes, Mr. Truman decides while Congress tries to get advantage in the election this fall. He decides while we're busy looking over the latest basketball scores or planning next summer's vacation. But we are the ones who will wake up disillusioned when the test comes. And we'll suffer the consequences unless we as voters demand that the men we elect in Congress begin to assert our rights.

February 9, 1950

WHAT STARTED INFLATION?

There is a growing rift between the President and Congress because the President persists in blaming the law-making body for the shortcomings of the New Deal. The latest move on the part of the White House is to blame Congress for the impending "inflation" which is bound to come, because of the Administration's policy of pandering to organized labor and granting this specially favored group one wage increase after another — which is a sure road to inflation.

Congress has declined to subscribe to the philosophy that creating an artificial or real shortage of commodities by executive order, then rationing the scarcity, is a sound solution of our economic problems. A majority of Congressmen believe in the fundamental law of supply and demand, with limited governmental reservations, and in the principle of MORE PRODUCTION instead of LESS PRODUCTION.

The conflict between the President and Congress for the moment has drifted into an argument over the policy of "subsidies" to control prices, which means the taking of tax money out of the treasury and handing it over to processors, manufacturers and producers instead of stabilizing both commodities and wages. The promised "roll back" of farm prices which is urged by organized labor, is also involved in this controversy. The War Labor Board is constantly changing the "little steel formula" and raising wages of certain groups of organized labor, completely ignoring the great middle class, known as the white collar group, which is not organized to put pressure on Washington.

Admittedly, inflation is caused by too much buying power in the hands of the people — more money than goods available — but farm groups and certain Congressmen contend that the President seems willing to increase the buying power of labor groups without conceding the same privilege to farm groups or producers. They fail to see that there is any difference in the inflationary influence of money whether it be in the pockets of the farmer or laborer.

The President has told Congress and the country that he proposed to go ahead with his subsidy program roll back of farm prices regardless of what farm groups or Congressmen from agricultural states think, when it is generally admitted that such a course will be a sure road to inflation.

Now let's take a look at this thing called inflation (increased buying power) and see how it got started. The New Deal which has been none too thrifty or zealous about saving the taxpayer's money, started inflation when it permitted contractors to bid up prices on governmental contracts and approved the "cost-plus" policy. The New Deal encouraged inflation when it encouraged the 40-hour week and time and one-half for overtime when there was a shortage of manpower in the country.

The New Deal encouraged inflation when it permitted defense workers and other government employees to draw exorbitant wages, including the payment of union racket fees for the privilege of working for the government. The New Deal encouraged inflation when it drew government workers from the farm, factories and private industries and paid them exorbitant wages, while it denied this same right and privilege to private industry. The New Deal encouraged inflation when it permitted the willful and deliberate waste of lumber, steel and other critical materials in war contracts and used public funds to replace this profligate waste. The New Deal encouraged inflation when it picked out special labor groups (ignoring the white collar group) and increased their wages beyond the "Little Steel Formula," which was the standard or yard stick set up by the War Labor Board. The New Deal encouraged inflation when it employed at high wages 3,000,000 government clerks, stenographers, publicity directors, public relations officials, so-called efficiency experts and technicians to write complicated government regulations, formulas, questionnaires and letters to further confuse and perplex the tired, over-worked taxpayer on the home front who is working 50 or more hours a week (without overtime) struggling to keep his business from bankruptcy.

So it comes poor grace for the President or anyone else to charge Congress — the only remaining link between the people and their government — with being responsible for inflation. Every American citizen should search for the truth in this critical hour — because "the truth will make them free."

November 18, 1943

RETURN TO CONSTITUTIONAL GOVERNMENT

As the time approaches for the special session of Congress there is every indication that there is going to be some plain speaking by Congressmen on the reconversion problem.

Already in published statements and interviews some Congressmen have stated rather bluntly that it is important for the country to return to constitutional government and begin giving serious consideration to civilian needs and the employment of labor in private industry. As one Congressman expressed it, we have for four years properly turned the affairs of the country over to military needs, giving the army and Commander in Chief everything they have requested in men, money and materials to fight the war, but now that the war is won we should as soon as practicable get rid of war controls and free private business so it can with confidence go ahead, expand and employ labor.

The army told Congress it was responsible for winning the war, did not want any interference and got everything it demanded — and in some instances much more than the Congress and the people believed it needed to win the war. Military policies prevailed, we won the war at a cost of more than a million casualties, fighting on every battlefield throughout the world, built up a public debt of $300,000,000,000 and have stock piles, surplus material and unused balances which some Congressmen estimate as high as $100,000,000,000. However, there are still some voices crying for continued military authority and continued control by boards, bureaus and commissions — controls which virtually tell the people where to stand, where to sit and what to think. This is not the American way. The American people, schooled in an atmosphere of liberty and personal freedom, want to maintain a partnership with their government and want their public officials to be their servants and not their masters. These are fundamental principles interwoven into the fabric of our constitution by our forefathers and it is time to return that kind of government.

One of the fruits of war is loose living, indifference, lower moral standards and ideals and in some instances down-right dishonesty. One is reminded of the age in history of Diogenes, who walked the streets of Athens in broad daylight with a lighted lantern, looking for an honest man. In all ages the world has been searching for the TRUTH — and we have been told on high authority that if we know the truth, the truth will set us free. Yet who today can proclaim for a certainty what the TRUTH is about our country, its politics, its philosophy, its aims and ideals and its sincere relationship between the government and the people. If the people, in any degree, have become disillusioned and lost confidence in their government what is the cause and what is the cure? In the babble of tongues, the confusion of bureaus and conflicts of edicts, the plain citizen on foot does not know where he stands or what his duty is.

As examples of confusion and conflict in authority, one bureau says one thing and another bureau says another, each trying to maintain its authority and perpetuate its existence. People are told by those in authority that the draft will continue another year and also that it will be discontinued on V-J Day or when Congress meets. They are told that there is a shortage of gasoline and coal. They are told that it will be necessary to keep 8,000,000 men in uniform for a year for police duty and that it will take only 1,000,000 during the same time for police duty. We are told that we have won the war and made the world safe for democracy (the objective for which we fought) and at the same time we are told by others in authority that we did not win the war, that the peace treaty is no good, and that we must maintain in uniform millions of men and the greatest army, navy and air force the world has ever seen if we are to have future peace — and one weak-voiced citizen ventures to inquire: "What did we fight the war for?" What are the people to believe with all this babble of voices? Secrecy has its proper place in time of war, but in time of peace secrecy between the government and people has no proper place. Secrecy built up $50,000,000 worth of waste and $100,000,000,000 worth of stock piles and unexpended balances. Taxpayers have a right to know what becomes of their money. It's time now for Congress to take back its constitutional powers and give the government back to the people.

August 23, 1945

THE PRESIDENT AND THE SUPREME COURT

Lines are being drawn for one of the bitterest contests in the history of Congress when the President's proposal for changing the status of the Supreme Court comes before that body for consideration. Party lines will be split asunder and the battle will be comparable to the memorable senate debate over the League of Nations during President Wilson's administration. The question is so grave and carries with such far-reaching possibilities that it is challenging the attention of our foremost statesmen and scholars.

The opponents of the President's proposal will point out that no great emergency exists to call for such drastic action, and that the plan should be held in abeyance until time be allowed for debate and deliberation, and that procedure should take the regular course of amending the constitution. They will contend that for 15 years no president has asked for such powers, and that the legislative, executive and judicial branches of government should remain inviolate as set out by the framers of the constitution, which document has been referred to by the world's greatest statesmen as the best concept of a charter of Democracy which has been given to mankind. It will be pointed out further that the court should remain free from popular clamor and fear of the electorate, in its work of interpreting the constitution and measuring legislation passed by Congress. It will be contended that while the present chief executive might not abuse this added power, the precedent once established, might be abused by some future executive.

The proponents of the plan on the other hand will point out that there is too much delay in the court procedure and that as our justices reach the age of 70 they become too conservative and are not alert to the changing conditions of this complex and progressive age — that they should be more responsive to popular opinion and legislative enactment.

It is becoming more evident every day that this question will not be fought out on party lines, as many leading Democrats, senators and congressmen are taking definite stands in opposition to the President's proposal, especially as it applies to increasing the number of justices and arbitrarily retiring them at the age of 70 years. Many persons, however, agree to changes in court procedure, and expediting of the court's work, who are opposed to the more drastic proposal of interfering with the personnel and number of court justices.

The *Telescope* believes it unwise to follow the President's leadership regarding the arbitrary retirement age and the immediate adding of six justices to the Supreme Court, although we believe there is reason for changes in court procedures and the expediting of work of the court.

The *Telescope* does not believe an emergency exists justifying such drastic action as proposed. Certainly before such a change from our fundamental form of government is made, there should be due deliberation and careful study, and that we should follow the regular channels of amending the constitution, giving the electorate of the country a chance for expression upon the subject.

From the lips of Washington and Lincoln and other great leaders of our country we have been taught that our courts should be removed as far as possible from popular whims and passing fads, and not be required to examine election returns before making their decisions. The courts are the bulwark of our form of government which should be respected and in which the country should have confidence — as they guard the lives and property of 125,000,000 people, and under the bill of rights they have across the ages stood as the defender of the rights and liberties of the people.

Following the election four years ago, when the country was in the depths of a world-wide depression and needed leadership to bring order out of chaos, the *Telescope* took the position that it was logical and proper to follow the President — the commander-in-chief of the army and navy — in the battle "to lick the depression." The *Telescope* stated then that there should be but one national plan of action — one official plan — to bring the country through a crisis second only to that of the World War and that it was the duty of every citizen at that time to stand loyally back of the President in his projected program.

In those four years progress has been made and mistakes have been made, as might be expected, and the country today is beating back to normal times — just as all European countries worked their way out of the tragic aftermath of the World War.

The *Telescope* has been tolerant, and has tried to be fair in its attitude toward the administration in its very difficult task of bringing the country through the worst depression in its history, and it is the candid opinion of the writer that what the country most needs now is a "breathing spell" and a chance to use unmolested its great reserve power to bring the country the balance of the way through a great crisis.

To repeat, the *Telescope* does not believe any emergency exists to justify the President in making his unprecedented proposal for changing the Supreme Court of the United States in the manner outlined in his message to Congress.

March 7, 1936

IS AMERICA LOSING ITS WAY?

During the month of February each year the Nation's thoughts turn to two great Americans — George Washington and Abraham Lincoln — men with great minds, great visions and great souls, men who loved their country dearly and who gave it a full measure of their loyalty. The former is credited with having established the Union, and the latter with having preserved it.

Like others of our founding fathers, these two great Americans took the people into their confidence and discharged their duties with a singleness of purpose, placing the Nation's welfare ahead of personal and political gain. It was on this kind of a foundation that America was built. For 160 years America stood like the Rock of Gibraltar — upright before the world, respected and honored, the symbol of democracy and the envy of the free nations of the earth. America taught that in a democracy people derive their just powers from the consent of the governed, and welded together a Nation conceived in liberty and developed under the philosophy of free enterprise.

Here for a century and a half, in such an atmosphere, was built a Nation with the greatest liberty and freedom, the highest standard of living of any nation on earth. It was in this atmosphere, with such lofty ideals, that our forefathers wrote the Declaration of Independence, Constitution, and Bill of Rights, which was declared by some foreign governments to be the greatest Charter of Liberty ever penned by man.

Henry Clay declared he would rather be right than President. George Washington said the first duty of every American was to America, to do justice to all. Said Washington: "Let us raise here a standard to which wise and honest men can repair." "A government," Lincoln declared, "of, by and for the people, which should not perish from the earth." After the Civil War, out of his great heart, Lincoln said: "With malice toward none, with charity for all, with firmness in the right as God gives us to see the right, let us strive to finish the work we have begun and bind up the Nation's wounds."

It is a far cry across that century and a half of illustrious history to the present era of greed, immorality and crime. The country has been led down the primrose path to the brink of disaster by false leaders, ostensibly into the lands of milk and honey, upon promises of security if the people would give up some of their liberties, with the inevitable result that they are losing both their security and liberty.

Frankly, America seems to have lost some of its ideals, patriotism, and love of country which in the early days animated individual citizens and inspired them to a greater national pride and loftier spirit.

Our country and our world can well afford to turn their thoughts to such ideals and examples as these of George Washington at Valley Forge and Abraham Lincoln at Gettysburg.

February 23, 1950

GAMBLING IN WHEAT

The Nation is all set for a 900,000,000 bushel wheat crop, according to crop reporters, and Kansas is marked down to produce something over 200,000,000 bushels or nearly a fourth of the entire crop in the United States.

In the meantime the grain gamblers are busy pushing wheat prices down. All sorts of pretexts are used by the speculators to bear the wheat market, as well as other commodity markets. For example, last year, the United States produced only 850,-000,000 bushels of wheat, but the Chicago grain gamblers bought and sold 10,000,000,000 bushels. This is 12 times as much as the entire wheat crop, and represents nothing more or less than a poker game in which wheat is used as chips. The same system of gambling is used to sell corn, pork, cotton and other commodities.

For years Congress has tried to place restrictions around this type of practice, one of which requires actual delivery of the product purchased, but even this seems to have been unsuccessful, because the law is not enforced. The normal application of the law of supply and demand is bound to work, just as the law of gravitation cannot be repealed, but the frenzied buying and selling of commodities on the Chicago Board of Trade, which transactions are not represented by actual merchandise, and sales should be prohibited. The actual producers of wheat, and not the speculators in wheat, are the ones who should have the profit for their labor and effort.

If Secretary Wallace or Congress want to do something realistic to help the wheat farmer they will protect him from human wolves who infest the Chicago wheat pit at this time of the year and juggle with the farmers grain crop.

May 26, 1938

WHAT ARE AMERICA'S OBJECTIVES?

The vital issue at the present time, and the question which every loyal American is asking is: "What are our aims and objectives in the present war, about the Atlantic Charter and Four Freedoms, what about self-determination for the Little

Nations — in short, what are we fighting for?" This is a fair question and one which should be answered truthfully and frankly to the American people, in view of the confusion and conflicting statements which are coming from the press and from high officials in Allied quarters.

Joseph Stalin has not hesitated to speak for Soviet Russia and Prime Minister Churchill has not hesitated to speak for Great Britain — at least as to some of their aims and objectives, and they have spoken so frankly that Washington official and diplomatic circles have been shocked. For example, Joseph Stalin has spoken quite frankly, and it may be said independently, about what he wants in Poland, Italy, Czechoslovakia, Finland and some of the Balkan countries, which do not square with the Atlantic Charter, the Moscow reference, the Casablanca and Teheran agreements. Mr. Churchill has said quite frankly that he had no intention of "liquidating the British Empire" and has stood adamant on the Indian-Palestine question, the Italian, Spanish and French problems, which are not entirely consistent with the United Nations, policies enunciated at previous conferences.

When President Roosevelt, at a press conference, told the world that we intended to divide the Italian fleet into three parts, giving Russia one-third (presumably for appeasement) the statement immediately brought sharp criticism from Italian and English quarters and an official statement by Churchill, qualifying and correcting what he called the Allied position. These repercussions caused the English Parliament the other day to demand of Mr. Churchill a clarification of the Atlantic Charter and other commitments which had been made by the United Nations. Mr. Churchill declined at the time to do so.

The American people have inquired from time to time about the commitments which have been made at the various conferences of Allied leaders and have been assured that there has been complete harmony and that the Allied nations see "eye to eye" in their aims and objectives. In view of some recent developments in the progress of the war, and statements of a conflicting nature emanating from high sources, many Americans are becoming confused and disillusioned and would like a frank statement by their government and a re-appraisal of our aims and objectives. They do not want to blunder to the peace table with no plan or program and sign a blank agreement and let the other parties to the contract write into the agreement whatever they wish. Chamberlain, trustful and altruistic, journeyed to Munich at Hitler's request, got into a poker game where they play for keeps, and not only lost his umbrella, but also lost the peace.

The American people stand where they have always stood, for an orderly world and are willing to contribute their share in sweat and blood and tears, toward the establishment of some international authority which will have power to maintain the peace, not only for big nations, but also for little nations — and the American people have no ulterior motives, want no territorial gain, and have held a dream of self-determination for weaker countries, and a belief that this would be a war to end war. If these ideals cannot be attained, then what are we fighting for? But now, as always, eternal vigilance is the price of liberty.

March 30, 1944

WHY NOT MAKE U.N. WORK?

Facing one of the gravest crises in the history of a nation, without forceful leadership, we are drifting, like a ship without a rudder, in the direction of World War No. Three. Without a chart or a compass or a coherent plan the people have become anxious, confused, deeply cynical and disillusioned at the course into which the country is drifting. Piece-meal pronouncements and fragments of policies have been issued from time to time by Washington departments and agencies, which have been unofficial and contradictory and have added to the confusion and lack of public confidence.

Belatedly, as usual, seven months after the signing of the United Nations' Charter, in response to mounting public clamor for its recognition and enforcement, James F. Byrnes, Secretary of State, makes the first definite, concrete pronouncement of United States policy in international affairs, adhering to the principles of United Nations Charter. Broadly speaking, this reflects popular opinion in this country. This long overdue pronouncement came after irreparable damage had been done to American prestige in world affairs by permitting, without effective protest, political economic chaos to develop throughout the world without exercising our well known world leadership.

After seven long months of vascillation and impotence we have seen various provisions of the United Nations Charter violated and principles of the Atlantic Charter, Yalta Agreement and Potsdam compact flaunted. We have seen boundary lines illegally changed, Little Peoples liberties and property rights exploited by political intrigue and international power politics. This is a far cry from the days last summer at San Francisco when fifty-one of the leading nations of the world solemnly signed a compact and pledged their sacred honor to adhere to a new world order which would substitute peaceful and humane means for settling international problems instead of the barbaric practice of war. Among the provisions of the U. N. was freedom, justice and equality for Little Nations and their right to self-determination in setting up their own governments.

All this had the ring of sincerity and it seemed to offer new hope to a tired and stricken world. It pointed to an era when nations would beat their spears into pruning hooks and their swords into plow shares. General MacArthur, military leader and top commander in the Pacific, referring to the accomplishments at San Francisco, said: "This is the world's last great hope and chance for peace."

At the very pinnacle of success and at the height of our power and prestige, when all nations, big and little, looked to the country of Washington and Lincoln, the country of liberty and justice, for leadership—we faltered and failed to supply that leadership. Frankly, how could we assist in the moral regeneration of other people unless we stopped the moral degeneration at home?

Following the adoption of the San Francisco Charter what did America do? Military voices were heard throughout the land, demanding big armies, big navies, super air forces and universal military training in peace time, presumably to fight the "next war." How did this fit into the solemn engagements just concluded at San Francisco and the new pattern of world order which was to be substituted for war, and how would the world at large receive such unexplained behaviour? It was a definite invitation and gesture for another world race in armaments.

Where was there any reassuring voice coming out of the nation's Capitol offering hope and comfort for the new world order, or even suggesting plans for making the United Nations Charter work? Ninety per cent of all the clamor in Washington official circles was for building up bigger and better armaments.

Militarists in this country and our nation's leaders can well take heed to the injunctions of our forefathers, who warned against international intrigues, and entangling alliances with foreign countries. We need a rededication in this country of American ideals—we need a clearer vision of Washington at Valley Forge and Lincoln at Gettysburg.

March 7, 1946

SAN FRANCISCO PEACE CONFERENCE

Momentous decisions will be made at San Francisco next month when delegates representing 44 nations will meet to decide the future destiny of the world. A good start was made at Dumbarton Oaks and progress was made in the recent conference of South American Republics at Mexico City when they pledged united action in case of aggression from within or without.

Some controversial questions have been carried over from Dumbarton Oaks to the San Francisco conference and one of these is the voting power of the various nations, which is vital and goes to the heart of the plan. At Dumbarton Oaks, Russia would not agree to a "majority rule" or any other majority percentage, Joe Stalin sticking to the theory that each of the Five Big Powers has the power to VETO any question affecting its vital interests or what might be called its "sovereign rights." This veto power, in the opinion of most of the delegates to Dumbarton Oaks conference, would nullify the effectiveness of the whole peace plan. However, Stalin stood adamant and, finally, at the Yalta conference both Roosevelt and Churchill told the world that they had reached complete agreement with Russia. Later Churchill, on the floor of Parliament, told his country he had agreed to the veto principle of the Five Big Powers, and Roosevelt told a press conference, he had yielded on this point. Many of the small countries are objecting and the veto question will be one of the major issues at the San Francisco conference.

Under the Dumbarton Oaks plan all countries (or states as they are called) will have one vote in the parent organization, the General Assembly, but in the Security Council, which in effect is an executive committee, will rest all the power of enforcing the provisions of the newly formed league. The

Security Council consists of 11 members — the Big Four, and possibly France, and six members at large, selected by Security Council. The Big Five are permanent members and the other six will serve two years, being rotated. France, at present, seems to be a "problem child."

Naturally, the question arises in the minds of the small nations whether such a plan is democratic and whether the authority springs from the people or is handed down by the autocratic Big Five who are permanent members and whose veto power can never be curtailed. It might be mentioned that the Big Five are the United States, Great Britain, Russia, China and probably France.

The smaller countries, asking for more equitable treatment, point to the Atlantic Charter, handed to the world by Roosevelt and Churchill more than two years ago and held up as an ideal and sort of a Declaration of Independence promising them self-determination and the right to select their own governments. That idealistic picture was somewhat dimmed if not shattered, when Stalin began changing border lines and setting up "buffer states" in the Balkans. Likewise, Churchill clung to his original statement that he "had no intention of liquidating the British Empire" by giving up African colonies or handing Hong Kong back to the Chinese. The progress of the war by our aid had reached a stage where some of the allies became more independent in their declarations. Some countries began to ask, "What about the Atlantic Charter?" Churchill's answer was, "After all, the Atlantic Charter was only a guide and not a rule." Roosevelt's answer was, "The Atlantic Charter was only some notes scribbled on scraps of paper."

Considering the original ideals which took America into the war — to make the world safe for democracy — a great disillusionment came into the minds of millions of Americans when it began to dawn upon them that we would probably be obliged to compromise some of our ideals to "appease" some of our allies without sacrificing our "sovereign rights." Realistically viewing the whole problem, we realize now that having been drawn into this world conflagration we have the bear by the tail and cannot let loose — and must do our best to salvage all we can out of an embarrassing situation, but let us learn something from the lesson it has taught.

Never again will America trust other countries to keep the peace. The only way we can be sure that it will be kept is to become a party to the contract, however imperfect, and do the best we can in the future years to improve its provisions, making them coincide with the principles of justice and the rule of law.

America, with its powerful influence, must furnish leadership in the new world order. Nearly every nation in the world today is insolvent and dependent upon America for rehabilitation. The richest nation in the world, with the greatest potential wealth, the largest army, navy and air force, with 150 years of free government which is the envy of other nations, this country has an obligation and a destiny to furnish leadership to a broken and impoverished world.

Having placed 12,000,000 men in uniform, suffered 1,000,000 in casualties, and having obligated future generations to a war debt of $300,000,000,000, and promised the people of the world liberty and security, America must not shirk its responsibility and leadership.

March 29, 1945

ANOTHER RACE IN ARMAMENTS

If this country follows the course mapped out by extreme militarists and echoed by President Truman, who does not want to relinquish his war time powers, we are in for the greatest armament race in history, declares John M. Hightower, writer for the Associated Press.

Before the ink is dry on the United Nations Charter and without giving this peace document, in which the world has pinned its faith, a chance to work, military influences in this country are trying to create war hysteria and rush the people into a huge military program, unprecedented in the nation's history, which would cost $5,000,000,000 and which cannot be justified by any sound basis of reasoning. Such a proposal ignores the Dumbarton Oaks conference, the Atlantic Charter, the Yalta agreement and makes a mockery out of the San Francisco Charter, which has been solemnly signed and ratified by all participating nations. In a nation-wide address the other day when the President flouted all our peace efforts, which have been the hope of the war-weary world and declared: "Peace must be built on power," he dashed the hopes of millions of subjugated people who have looked forward with faith to this country, believing we would assume the leadership in taking the world out of the barbaric practice of war. Top ranking militarists, who live in a military atmosphere, and military-minded Congressmen, have systematically tried to build up a war psychology and it has temporarily influenced the thinking of the President and some of the people.

Both General MacArthur and General Eisenhower, who are doing a fine job restoring peace in their respective spheres, and have practical knowledge of civilian as well as military affairs, have told the country that there is no threat of war in the foreseeable future, and that Germany and Japan are completely subjugated militarily and economically. We still have nearly 8,000,000 men in uniform, with no military threat from any quarter and the United States is the only solvent nation in the world. Frankly, there are only two powers in the world who could, by any stretch of the imagination, be considered potential economic enemies, and they are begging the United States today for billions of dollars to rehabilitate their countries. In the face of such conditions it does not make sense for this country to suddenly abandon peaceful efforts, now in the process of being tried, and tell the world 'Force' is the only power that can be recognized, thereby suggesting a race in armaments.

What a disillusionment this must be to the American people, who were told that this was a war to end war, a war to make the world safe for democracy, and were solemnly promised that American boys would not fight on foreign soil. How can the government and men in authority reconcile these things with present military proposals and make them square with the Atlantic Charter, Yalta agreement and San Francisco Charter? A leading educator cannot reconcile our position in disarming Germany and Japan, destroying their war text books and teaching them the ways of peace, while we propose to abandon our present educational system in high schools, colleges and universities and teach the youth of the country the arts of war in West Point and Annapolis. While the President proposes to take out the normal lives of our youth only one year for military training, Admiral King told the country Saturday that on account of the atomic bomb and other modern weapons, it should call for at least 18 months of military training for the youth of the country. This would mean that we are to take the youth of the land out of the home with its ideals and wholesome influence and place them in army camps with the influence and environment which usually goes with such an abnormal life. It is admitted that the atomic bomb has completely revolutionized the problem of national defense and introduced the potency of science and technology. Present methods of warfare are completely outmoded and the training of soldiers in routine army tactics for a year or eighteen months would be completely wasted. Any physical training needed can be secured in high schools and colleges and certainly such limited training they would get in army camps would have no technical value five or ten years hence.

Nobody in this country is advocating "pacifism." (This is just a catch word used by militarists to fool people.) Everybody in this country, so far as has been revealed, wants ADEQUATE NATIONAL DEFENSE, but they do not want to leave this responsibility to military-minded people who have given other groups but little opportunity to be heard in Washington. One high ranking military officer said if quick action was not had he was afraid the country would grow cold on the subject. The people have a right to expect their Congressmen, who are elected by the people, to give full and impartial appraisal of the whole question of national defense without being rushed into such a gigantic program with all its implications. Why not also give the boys in uniform some voice in the matter? They know more about war and the needs of the country militarily than do some of the swivel-chair Generals in the Pentagon Building.

Senator Edwin C. Johnson, born in Republic County, head of the military affairs committee, who is opposed to such a program, says no matter what kind of sugar-coated name is given the plan it is still "conscription." Congressman Bennett of Missouri said: "Before militarism is saddled upon the country I would like to see the Administration use its influence to induce other countries to abandon universal military training." Winston Churchill, speaking in Commons the other day, said: "The task of holding Germany down will not be as hard a task as holding Germany up." Churchill further said: "The R.A.F. should be reduced to a personnel of 40,000 and the navy should be brought back to pre-war strength." Obviously Churchill does not see the need of a big military establishment. The Kansas delegation in Congress, expressing the sentiment of the home people, has committed itself against universal military training in peace time as being a departure from our constitutional form of government and the principles of democracy.

Unless the people of this country become aroused to the dangers ahead—and how rapidly a military form of government is encroaching upon them and their civil liberties—they will wake up some day and find themselves in the clutches of military rule instead of civil government under our boasted democracy. Congress, the last remaining link between the people and their government, is their only recourse.

May 2, 1947

HERBERT HOOVER—CITIZEN, STATESMAN

An outpouring of citizens from Iowa and throughout the country at West Branch, Iowa, last week to honor the state's most distinguished native son on his eightieth birthday was a tribute few men live to experience. Hoover's speech on that occasion will go down in history alongside those of George Washington in his "Farewell Address' and Abraham Lincoln in his "Gettysburg Address."

Son of a West Branch blacksmith, orphaned at the age of 12 and self-supporting at the age of 15, he has given the world one more example of how far an American boy can go under our form of government. He has proven, once again, in this country of free enterprise that any citizen with a burning ambition can go as far as his skill and ability will carry him, without interference by his government.

Aside from the honors which have been heaped upon Hoover in this country, his appointment by President Woodrow Wilson, a Democrat, to administer the Belgian relief, in which he handled approximately one billion dollars is but one of his world services. He was the first Quaker to hold the high office of President. It was not known until years after he retired that he did not draw his salary as President—but left it to charity. He served as Secretary of Commerce under President Harding and continued in the cabinet under Calvin Coolidge. To recount his great services to his country would be an endless job—and his name will be written high on the scroll of fame by his countrymen as representing the highest and best in the American tradition.

When he took the office of President in 1929 one of the great newspapers of the country said of him: "He had executive ability of the highest order, his spiritual and moral qualities were above question, and he felt obligated to tell the truth as he saw it regardless of voter consequences."

One of the blackest chapters in American history is the campaign that followed when certain politicians set out to "get" President Hoover—by charging him with every conceivable political error, including the "bringing on of the depression," which, of course, was the aftermath of a world war dislocating commerce and industry throughout the world and piling up a huge public debt. The Quaker President took the charges tolerantly and tried to explain world conditions and domestic affairs with logic—but in the heat of a campaign the average voter does not always listen to logic. His political opponents employed the most prolific "ghost writers" and "hatchet men" available and conducted one of the most vicious political campaigns ever waged against a great citizen.

Governor George Hodges, Democratic governor of Kansas, was so incensed at the unfair and false attack on Hoover that he said: "Why blame Hoover for present economic conditions, created by the war; the official scolders in the East have lathered themselves into a white heat by making unfair charges; this rough stuff sent out by political agencies is not in accordance with the truth."

William Allen White, one of Kansas' greatest citizens and writers, was an admirer of Herbert Hoover and they have been guests in each other's homes. In a page one editorial in the *Emporia Gazette,* White called for a halt on the unfair treatment given by politicians and the Democratic press and said in one of his paragraphs: "No President since Grover Cleveland has been so unfairly abused as Herbert Hoover; he made a great President and has done a great service to the American people in handling the potential bank panic and other protective measures as an aftermath of the world war."

In my work as executive clerk of the United States Senate in two sessions of Congress I had occasion to meet this great man. My office handled special messages, diplomatic appointments, army and postoffice appointments which were transmitted under seals from the White House to my office for transmittal to the Senate for confirmation. I know him as one of our greatest Americans.

August 19, 1954

THE SOLDIERS' RIGHT TO VOTE

It seems most incredible that anyone would make the "picayune" charge that Congress is trying to prevent the soldiers from voting. No wonder our national legislators bitterly resented the implication by President Roosevelt, which stigmatized them not only before the soldiers, but before the American people as well. On the floors of Congress and in public interviews

Congressmen resented the charge, which they said not only questioned their motives but also their patriotism. The President challenged them to "stand up and be counted" on the soldiers' vote bill — and they did, and the vote in the House showed 215 votes for a state-rights bill as against 164 votes for the President's Federal bill. Bills which had been favorably considered by Congress gave the soldiers the right to vote, not only for the President and Congressmen, but also on state and local candidates, whereas the proposed Federal bill favored by the President permitted soldiers to vote only on President, Vice-President and members of Congress.

The exact language of the President's message to Congress, as quoted by the press was: "I consider this proposed legislation (state control) a fraud on the soldiers, sailors and marines now training and fighting for us and for our sacred rights — and a fraud upon the American people." This is a serious charge; it impugns the motives of Congress and stigmatizes them before the American people and the soldiers in uniform, smacks too much of politics — and certainly does not promote national unity.

Honestly, how many American people over three years of age actually think our Congressmen would pass a law to prevent soldiers from voting — or do any other thing to deny them their full sovereign rights as American citizens? It is presuming a lot on the credulity of the people to think they would believe such a serious charge. No wonder the Congressmen got fighting mad and resented such an implication, when they were trying to pass an absent-voting law, within the limitations of the Constitution, which would permit soldiers to vote not only on federal officers, but also on state and local candidates. It is the sworn duty of Congress to initiate and enact the laws and the sworn duty of the President to enforce the laws. One of the basic fundamental criticisms of the New Deal by Congress and the public generally has been the tendency of the executive branch of government to usurp powers belonging to the legislative branch of government.

Commenting on this surprising attack on Congress by the President at a time when national unity is so much desired, the *Kansas City Star* says editorially: "The President's blast at Congress on soldier vote legislation has contributed nothing to the solution of a complicated problem—on the contrary it has stirred up resentment and may serve to delay the kind of legislation that is needed and the kind that even Mr. Roosevelt himself would desire. Why then did the President come in with his charge of fraud," says the *Star,* "directed at the previous Senate bill and thus arouse Congressional resentment; obviously, it was to get Administration credit for what might be done in an effective way, and to shift responsibility for what might be done in another way."

February 10, 1944

THE RIGHT TO WORK

You have heard a lot in recent years about "the right to strike," but very little has been said about "the right to work." It's about time someone is appearing for the defense and making a plea for the millions of unorganized, honest workmen, skilled in many industries, who wish to work and support their families, but who do not belong to a labor union and pay dues to some radical labor boss who in some instances use the money to exploit the workmen.

Radical labor union leaders have been petted and coddled by the administration for many years until they have reached the point where they seem to think they are bigger than the government, and are actually challenging the government defense program in a great crisis and it is time the authorities in Washington crack down on this sort of racketeering.

If the government is strong enough to conscript men and materials and levy extraordinary taxes upon the people, it ought to be strong enough and virile enough to make radical labor leaders behave. The public has been asked to support the war effort 100 per cent and they have the right to demand that the government make labor in defense industries also support the defense program, without striking, thereby slowing down the program and refusing to let other Americans work in defense industries.

Figures show that three-fourths of the workmen of this country are independent and do not belong to labor groups and it is not just for the one-fourth minority to dictate to the government a working policy for the three-fourths majority. While we are talking about the four freedoms for people in all parts of the world, why not give a little attention to the four freedoms in our own country?

Senator Daniels of Texas has introduced a resolution for a constitutional amendment protecting the right of men to work. Why should it be necessary for a constitutional amendment in a democracy like ours, under our constitution and bill of rights, to permit and protect American citizens while taking their lunch boxes and going to their jobs without molestation on the part of any citizen or group of citizens? What's happened in this country that such a thing is tolerated? Grover Cleveland saw to it that men were protected in this country in their right to work and Teddy Roosevelt saw to it that the United States mails moved in a threatened strike, and Calvin Coolidge saw to it that the Boston police "did not strike against the government," as he called it.

More than 15,000,000 man-days of labor have been lost in this country recently on account of strikes, and millions of men have been kept out of jobs who want to work, and it's time the government sees to it that all American citizens are protected in their constitutional rights to work without the necessity of passing a constitutional amendment.

November 20, 1941

WHAT TOURIST TRAFFIC IS WORTH

Entirely aside from the fact that Kansas should complete her highway system for local and economic reasons, the state should also complete the trunk-line roads because Kansas is losing several million dollars annually in gasoline receipts and expenditures from tourists who are routed around the state because of wide gaps and dirt detours on some of Kansas' important federal highways.

The National Park Service has just given out figures showing what tourist traffic is worth to the various states. The total amount of money spent by tourists in the United States last year, according to this government department, was $5,003,100,000. New York received the largest amount, $846,800,000 and California next with an income from tourists of $416,800,000. Missouri received from tourists last year $138,200,000, while Kansas is credited with only $80,050,000. Both states are strategically located in the geographical center of the United States, on substantially the same east-west federal highways and should carry approximately the same east-west travel, providing the trunk-line highways are in equal condition. However, the thing that happened was that through travel was routed around Kansas — via Nebraska and Oklahoma — because the Kansas highway system was not completed and because of dirt detours.

This situation should be corrected and some plan evolved to complete the Kansas federal road system at an early date. At present nearly one-half the total revenues of the highway department are spent for maintenance. The coming session of

Elwood M. Brooks, President of Central National Bank and Trust Company of Denver, and Edwin C. Johnson, two native Kansans and co-workers of Miller in the drive for good roads.

PHOTO COURTESY DENVER POST

the legislature should undertake to adopt some sound, economic plan which will complete the state's road system without so much waste and so much political log rolling. If the highway commission was placed under civil service, or at least their tenure of office lengthened, and the commssion was permitted to follow sound engineering advice instead of political advice, the state would soon have a connected system of roads, based upon traffic count and use to which the roads are subjected.

W. L. Elson, of Pratt, secretary of the Kansas Hotel association, says that most states have seen to it that their trans-state roads, are in good condition, and that twenty-six states have legislative appropriations, promoting outside travel within their borders. These states hold that such advertising is of sound economic value and an investment, because it increases gasoline revenue within the state as well as promoting tourist expenditures. In this connection this association has given out figures of tourist expenditures. The tourist dollar is divided as follows: Twenty-five cents for retail purchases, such as clothing, drugs, souvenirs, etc. Twenty-one cents for food. Ten cents for garage and tire service. Twenty cents for hotel, tourist camp and other lodging. Eight cents for amusements. Ten cents for gasoline and oil. Six cents for miscellaneous.

These figures are based upon a daily expenditure of $10 per tourist. If they are correct and if Kansas actually collects $80,050,000 from the tourists and Republic county received its share it would mean $800,000 annually to the county. This is more than the value of the county wheat crop this year and four times as much as the value of the corn crop. Whatever the amount the tourist spends annually in Kansas it is an impressive sum, and the fact that other states organize to go after it and spend thousands of dollars annually to attract the tourist is sufficient reason to cause Kansas to pay some attention to the subject.

In this connection the *Telescope* desires to direct the attention of the highway department to the deplorable condition of one of the state's major trunk-line federal roads — U. S. 36 — which has been neglected for more than ten years and has never been brought to standard federal grade or surface, and for this reason thousands of tourists are routed through Nebraska. All states east of Kansas have paved this important highway and Colorado has constructed the road with standard grade, bridges and culverts and is now surfacing the route. When completed it will reduce the mileage between Indianapolis and Denver more than 200 miles and Kansas is the only state which has failed to bring the road to federal specifications.

June 17, 1948

N. C. K. FREE FAIR A MODERN MIRACLE

I sat in the grandstand at the North Central Kansas Free Fair last week and witnessed the fruits of a modern miracle — the result of years of hard labor and cooperation of a civic-minded community. I saw the fruits of nearly fifty years of persistent efforts (in good years and bad years) matured into the third largest agricultural, livestock and amusement program in the state. The standard of measurement or yard stick used in this case is that of attendance, quality and quantity of livestock and agricultural exhibits, 4-H club art, and domestic economy exhibits, last and by no means least, the amusement program furnished by the Chamber of Commerce fair amusements committee.

More than a third of a century ago the Republic County fair, like hundreds of other local fairs, during a period of dry years and depression years, went broke — but the seeds for a successful fair remained, were replanted, matured and blossomed into what thousands of people saw at the N. C. K. Free Fair last week. And in this connection it should be noted that the basic reason for the growth and development of this great central Kansas enterprise is the splendid cooperation across the years between the County Fair Board and the Belleville Chamber of Commerce. Nearly forty years ago when the primitive fair association "folded up" a meeting of the Board of County Commissioners and Chamber of Commerce was held and both agreed the enterprise should be carried on. The County Fair Board agreed to take over both the assets and liabilities of the old fair association, which included real estate and buildings. The County Board was to continue to operate, under the law, the agricultural and livestock departments, receiving a subsidy from the state, while the local Chamber was to develop and operate the amusement program. The old fair committee started with a crude grandstand with a seating capacity of from 500 to 600 and the amusement program consisted of horse racing and harness races. Today the Fair Association of Republic County owns more than $100,000 worth of real estate and buildings, built and paid for by both the Chamber of Commerce Fair amusements committee and the County Fair board. Today with two huge grandstands and bleachers, with a capacity of 5,000, sees an overflow crowd every year. Last year the Fair amusements committee completed modern rest rooms in one of the three grandstands, costing more than $10,000 and is considering a cover over the large bleacher section soon. Today the North Central Kansas Free Fair is credited with having the fastest half-mile banked dirt race track in the country on which several auto race track records have been broken. The experiment this year by adding horse races proved to be popular with the public. Also "The Vogues of Manhattan," a stage show, costing approximately $6,000, proved a popular attraction. The 4-H Club program and exhibits has developed into one of the most popular features of the fair programs. And it should not be overlooked that the city of Belleville cooperates each year with its municipal electric lights and the city sprinkler to keep down the dust and to bring the oval dirt race track to a point of perfection for racing. Finally, it may be said, this annual agricultural, livestock and amusement program is an example of what a community can do when all agencies and the people work together in a common effort to promote a worth-while community program.

September 9, 1954

IDEALS AND OBJECTIVES OF SERVICE CLUB

What is a service club worth to a community? The value depends entirely upon the personnel or individual members of the club in carrying out its objectives; its value to the community depends upon the amount of energy and work the club members are willing to put into the job.

The writer knew Belleville when it had no service club, no Chamber of Commerce, no community group where men could meet around a table, bury their prejudices and think and plan for the greater community interest. Everybody was trying to take a "free ride" and contribute nothing. It was a free-for-all contest, Texas rules, no holds barred and the devil take the hindmost. In those pioneer times, known as the "horse and buggy days," Belleville thought it could get along with dirt streets, board sidewalks and no street lighting except kerosene lamps. It had no sewer system, inadequate and antiquated school facilities and the city's water supply came from a shallow dug well in the court house square. The city government was just as antiquated as the other city standards and there was no progressive leadership — except the feeble efforts of its newspaper and a few far-sighted citizens. When the first Chamber of Commerce was organized, more than 40 years ago (called the Commercial Club) it attained a peak membership of 71 and the dues were $1.00 a year—and that was its budget. The Commercial Club campaigned for cement sidewalks on Main street, for an adequate water system, sewer system, street lighting and paving and for improved and modern educational facilities. The "city fathers" reacted favorably to the awakened progressive spirit and shortly the Lion's club was formed to help carry the community forward.

A community is not better or worse than the ideals and objectives carried out by its civic clubs, Chamber of Commerce and city administration and these are the things which reflect the spirit and life of the community.

What then should be the ideals and objectives of every live, progressive community? Let one of the greatest civic leaders of the country, who has just been elevated to the highest position nationally in his club, tell the story. We'll call him "George" and his club may be any one of a half dozen service clubs serving their communities: "Every man approaches the problem he faces with the kind of thinking he knows best. The lawyer thinks in terms of principle and precedent, the painter in terms of aesthetic values, the grocer in terms of supply and demand. I have spent most of my life in chemistry and find my thoughts turning to some of the thoughts and formulas with which I am most familiar. One of the marvels of chemistry is the catalyst which is a substance that speeds up chemical action. I think of my service club as a catalyst.

"I see it as one of the most effective accelerators of desirable action in the great field of human relations. You have watched it work as I have. Here is a man. He has good impulses and high energy—but does nothing with them. Then, suddenly, by the catalytic action those two virtues interact in him, and next we see him on his Chamber of Commerce board, in crippled-children work, at meetings of his trade associations.

"And here is a town divided against itself — the North End versus the South End, or the Arabs versus the Jews, or the Moslems versus the Hindus. In comes a service club, drawing business and professional men from both groups to its friendly board. Gradually the rivals drop their guard, warm to each other, and soon begin working side by side to produce the unity that makes a town a community.

"In one respect a service club is quite different from the catalysts of chemistry. We know exactly how it works. There is no mystery about it. Clubs begin with acquaintance, with simple friendship — with a kind of fellowship so basic that a man's political or religious beliefs make no difference. In that atmosphere the clubs hold before the man the principle of 'Service above Self' and encourages him to practice it in all his human contacts. It conceives of the individual club as a training ground for leaders for the long crusade to raise business standards, improve community well-being, and enlarge the total of world understanding. It is as simple as that.

"What, then, shall we do with our formula during the next 12 months? Let it be our foremost aim this year to promote friendliness, tolerance, cooperation — in other words, understanding — among all peoples. This we begin at home. We have seen the infant United Nations round out its first year of life. Let us work even harder than in the past to see that the aims and achievements of this organization on which 51 nations have pinned their hopes for a secure world are understood. This we begin at home — in our club programs, our fireside groups, our publications, our conversations. Only if each national an informed public opinion actively works for peace can we avoid international anarchy that would spell the end of civilization as we know it.

"Let us reemphasize helpfulness. I know no better way of saying it. Let us this year measure our progress by the yardstick of the service that we render to our fellowmen.

"The most serious danger that confronts our society today is the decline of moral values. The Roman Empire collapsed not because of the barbarian hordes, but because of the moral decay which was gnawing from within. Let us fight the moral decline which has gone so far in so many places today. Let us strive to restore honor and integrity to their high places."

May 8, 1947

FREEDOM OF THE PRESS

Because the present national administration has not earned the confidence and support of the newspapers of this country — both dailies and country weeklies — Governor Stevenson lashed out at the American press in an Oregon speech, charging that the press of the country did not represent the sentiments of the people. President Truman in a press conference in Washington later reiterated Governor Stevenson's charges. The country is familiar with the President's attack not only on the press but also on Congress, the legislative body elected by the people, as well as his personal attacks upon reputable public citizens who disagree with the Administration's socialistic tendencies, graft and public waste, not to mention unbearable taxes which will have to be paid by our children and grandchildren.

While both Governor Stevenson and President Truman criticize the press of the country for not seeing the "light," they carefully hide from the public mention of the tons of publicity printed and mailed out monthly by scores of government bureaus at taxpayers' expense by hundreds of publicity men and thousands of employees praising the work of these duplicated and useless bureaus.

Frankly, it is not an accident, but there is a reason why an overwhelming majority of the newspapers, magazines, commentators and editorial writers of the country cannot approve the type of administration which this country has been subjected to in recent years — and declare "It's time for a change."

Any thoughtful citizen knows it is the duty and obligation of the press of the country to support public officials and public measures which, in their opinion, are for the general welfare of the country and which conform to the constitution and bill of rights, as conceived and written in blood by our forefathers. In critical times like these when the peace of our country is in jeopardy and the financial insolvency of our country is being stretched to the breaking point, it is fortunate indeed that, under our bill of rights, we still have free speech and a free press to warn the people of excesses on the part of public officials who might for political reasons, lead us into pathways inimical to the public welfare.

David Lawrence, one of the great journalists and economists of the country, speaks out in defense of constitutional government and excesses by ambitious politicians. Here are some of Mr. Lawrence's comments:

"The Illinois governor says he doesn't know why most of the newspapers editorially have been against Democrats."

"In the first place, this statement is not true. The press has never been against Democrats as such but against candidates and office holders who call themselves Democrats but who are in reality faithless to their party history and to original creed of Thomas Jefferson.

"No other administration in history has had the benefit of millions of dollars of taxpayers' money for press agents, radio experts, information specialists and press relations officers. Day by day and week after week, they have poured forth a stream of publicity in the guise of "Official" news which has given many a person a lopsided view of controversial subjects.

"There is no such thing as an opposition publicity bureau by the Republicans or anybody else between presidential campaigns.

"Governor Stevenson may not know it, but the trend of editorial expression opposed to the 'New Deal' and the 'Fair Deal' has not been due to any feeling of dislike for the Democratic Party as such but is really a protest against the propaganda of the scheming individuals who have taken over the Democratic Party.

"If the Republican Party gets in and goes wrong, it, too, will earn the opposition of the press. This is proved in dozens of state and local elections during the last 20 years where Republican newspapers have fought Republican machines and their candidates.

"The American Press traditionally has defended the liberty of the individual and his right to save his earnings. That's why it has lined up again and again in opposition to the confiscationists, whether they seek to destroy liberty by "packing" the Supreme Court of the United States or by spending the savings of the country with the excuse that they are benefiting social welfare.

"The Democratic presidential nominee said in his Oregon speech that many newspapers had jumped to the support of General Eisenhower even before they knew what the Democratic platform or who the candidate would be. That's right, because most everybody knew in advance that the Democratic nominee would have to stand on the Truman record and most of the newspapers, after more than three years of observation, had already made up their minds that a vote for the Democratic nominee, no matter how good he himself might be, was merely a vote to approve and vindicate one of the most irresponsible administrations in American history."

September 18, 1952

CHAPTER X

Outstanding Kansas' Personalities

"Some Men Help Build a Better World, Others Come Along and Live In It"

EVERY man's life is touched by personalities of stature who profoundly impress him and shape his life. During his sixty-odd years as a Kansas journalist, A. Q. Miller knew many such men, some of whom are recorded in this chapter.

Quin Miller has revealed in his personal correspondence and other writings the influence these men exercised on him and on his beloved Kansas. In gleaning this information no attempt is made to chronicle these personalities' biographies in detail but enough information is related to give readers an idea of what kind of men were associated with Quin Miller during his busy career as a country editor, and how he has cherished their friendship over the years.

Some of these men have achieved national prominence; others are little known outside Kansas. Quin Miller did not use prominence as the yardstick for measuring friendship. His friends are those men who gave of themselves in the interest of their fellow

Dr. Raymond V. Kearns, former pastor of the First Presbyterian Church of Salina, now a member of the Church's National Division of Evangelism. Kearns in addition to being Miller's spiritual advisor, remains a close personal friend. Miller was privileged to fill in on a Preacher's Foursome at Salina's Golf Course and recalls that Kearns referred to himself as a Civil War golfer "out in 64 back in 65."

citizen. They are men whose integrity and devotion to their duty, as they saw it, made their lives rich and therefore adequate reward for adhering to these ideals.

No biography of A. Q. Miller would be complete without paying some tribute to these individuals. His sentiment can be expressed adequately only by his own statement.

"Space does not permit mention of all the fine men and women with whom I was privileged to associate during my many years as a Kansas editor. But I would like to pay special tribute to these men who are an integral part of my biography. I say this because they exercised an influence on me that guided and shaped my life, politically and spiritually. Some of these men have passed away, but whether living or dead their contribution to society will live on."

Harvey H. Motter, Businessman, Public Official

Some years ago a discussion before the Salina Gridiron Club was around the subject: "What individual has most influenced your life?"

Quin Miller answered: "Harvey H. Motter, Collector of Internal Revenue."

How much Motter meant to A. Q. Miller is indicated in the fine editorial he wrote at the time of his beloved friend's death.

"In the passing of Harvey H. Motter, Kansas has lost one of its most beloved and useful citizens. With an understanding heart and unfailing desire to serve across the years of his active life, Harve Motter ministered in a thousand ways to the manifold needs and comforts of his fellow men.

"A devoted Christian and a loyal Rotarian, he exemplified their code 'service before self,' thereby finding expression for the great love which was in his heart for his fellow man. His untiring energy, great ability and unfailing resourcefulness were exerted constantly to ennoble the lives of others. Unselfish in his personal desires, he could have risen to greater political heights had he employed the ruthless tactics sometimes used by practical politicians.

"As collector of internal revenue and in other positions of responsibility, he collected and disbursed millions of dollars of public money without a breath of suspicion ever being cast in his direction—and he died, as he desired, a poor man in material wealth but rich in the hearts of the people.

"As chairman of the Republican state central committee he refused to accept campaign contributions from certain sources which he thought might later embarrass his party. As collector of internal revenue he instilled into the service that humanitarian spirit which was exemplified so well in his own life and substituted for hard-boiled collection practices, the spirit of the Golden Rule. He admonished his subordinates never to take a penny that did not belong to the government, advised them always to take pains to see that the taxpayer was given all of his legal rights. It was his policy to pursue a claim for the refund of money to the taxpayer with the same diligence with which collections were made.

"An example of his democratic spirit and sincere love for his fellowmen was brought forcibly to my attention when he was appointed collector of internal revenue by President Harding. A reception and dinner had been arranged for him by influential political and business friends at Wellington and he invited the writer to accompany him. When we arrived at Wellington, he did not pay his first visit, as might be expected, to the chairman of the committee or the banker or the editor, but he wanted first to greet his old Greek friend, proprietor of a candy kitchen.

"Over a period of years Harve Motter could call more Kansans by their first names than any other citizen and in his public and private work he always had time to greet his callers and listen sympathetically to their problems. One of the great joys he gained from life was the ability to render a service or do a good deed for a friend. Like Lincoln, he loved the common people and without ostentation spent much time ministering to them.

"He was a 'natural-born' organizer and administrator had a great capacity for work and always put system and efficiency into his job. Likewise he had a great capacity for true friendship.

"My life was made richer and fuller because of contacts and fellowship with Harve Motter — because of his radiant personality his homely philosophy and his lofty ideals. He was an inspiration to thousands of men to do better work and live better lives. The world is better because Harve Motter sojourned in it for a brief period."

Charles F. Scott, Journalist and Statesman

"I knew Charley Scott as a journalist; I knew him as a politician and statesman; I knew him on the golf course. He was always a gentleman and could contribute something important and constructive to any conversation. Others may have had more of this world's goods but none left a richer heritage of friendship.

"Senator Capper once said: 'Charlie Scott is one of the ablest and most courageous men Kansas ever had in public life.' This after Scott had failed to support Capper for governor on the Bull Moose ticket.

"Politically, Charlie Scott wanted to know if a thing was morally and ethically right as well as economically sound. He did not ask: 'can it be done?' but rather 'should it be done?' Born and reared in Kansas and a graduate of Kansas University, Scott was a veteran of the first World War. He became a world traveler and lecturer and was elected to the Kansas Senate before representing his state as Congressman-at-Large.

"When the Redpath-Horner summer Chautauquas were popular fare during the first decade of the twentieth century one of the most popular political offerings was a debate between Charlie Scott and Henry Allen, two of the state's most popular orators. Scott represented the conservative Republican stand and Allen spoke for the Progressives. Following a particularly heated debate one summer in Belleville, Scott suggested that Allen and I accompany him to the local soda fountain. On the way Henry Allen remarked: 'Charlie, I believe you got the best of it today, judging from the applause.'

" 'Well, I think you had the best of the audience yesterday,' replied Scott.

"Then they both concluded that the people were partial to Scott because they read the editorials in the *Belleville Telescope.*

"In 1928 Charley Scott ran for nomination as Governor of Kansas and I was active in the campaign. Scott was not nominated but continued his active interest in the politics of the state and the nation.

"As editor of the *Iola Register,* Charlie Scott influenced my political thinking to a great extent. I was born a conservative and in my early days as a journalist believed that everything that existed was right and that change was experimental, dangerous and revolutionary. Charlie Scott was a conservative, too, but not quite as extreme as I was. His opinions helped to mellow my thinking and taught me to get the facts from both sides.

"Scott's friendship was valued by the non-conservative element, too. Harold Chase, liberal editor of the *Topeka Daily Capital,* in writing me about an editorial I had written concerning him and Scott stated: 'I appreciate being identified with Charlie Scott as working sincerely for what I believe. Scott is one of the finest men in Kansas'."

Arthur Capper — Printer, Publisher, Statesman

"One of my finest memories is that of nearly sixty years of friendship with the inimitable Arthur Capper. I knew him first

The late Arthur Capper, Kansas publisher, Governor of his State, and United States Senator, one of Kansas' most distinguished citizens.

as a printer on J. K. Hudson's old *Topeka Capital.*

"Arthur Capper started to learn the printing trade as a boy, working in the back shop of his home town newspaper, the *Garnett Review,* for one dollar a week. His Quaker parents had taught him the ways of temperance and thrift. When Capper was thirteen he wrote an article for a youth journal published in Topeka. This article is deserving of mention because in it the youthful Capper indicates his determination to succeed.

" 'A young man, a printer by trade, told me when I commenced to learn the trade, that it was the poorest trade there was, and that I could not make a living at it. I do not think that it can be the poorest trade. Since I have been at this trade, I find that a great many printers chew, smoke and drink. I am now thirteen years old and I am going to try and put my savings out at interest in place of spending them for tobacco and drinks. And by the time I am twenty-one do you think I will have enough money to buy a good second-hand press or will it turn out as the young man I mentioned said, that printing was the poorest trade in America.'

"Arthur Capper went on to prove that printing was not the 'poorest trade in America.' He purchased the *North Topeka Mail* and later the *Kansas Breeze.* Consolidating the two papers he retained Tom McNeal, of the *Breeze,* as editor. Capper remained in charge of the mechanical department. The *Mail & Breeze* became one of the state's outstanding newspapers.

"During a hot political campaign, in the days of Populism, the *Mail & Breeze* offered a $20.00 prize 'for the best cartoon on a political subject.' Albert Reid, a printer on the *Clyde Voice,* won the prize. Reid started on the road to fame as an artist and cartoonist with the winning of this prize.

"Arthur Capper did not enter the political field until he was 47 years of age. At that time few realized that he would serve four years as governor of Kansas and 30 years as a member of the United States Senate. Capper lost his first election race and I was a member of his opposition.

"In 1912, Arthur Capper joined the Bull Moose movement, headed by Teddy Roosevelt and ran for Governor of Kansas, on the Republican ticket. William Howard Taft was the Republican presidential nominee and, I felt, should have been supported by Capper. I wrote Capper and told him frankly that my newspaper could not support him for governor under those circumstances but that my conscience would not allow me to vote for his opponent.

"Many leading newspaper men were in favor of the third "Bull Moose" party; Arthur Capper, William Allen White, Joe Bristow, Victor Murdock and W. R. Nelson. But the *Belleville Telescope* supported William Howard Taft.

"When Capper received my letter he replied with his characteristic attitude: 'he hoped this would not cause a break in our friendship.' While there was a 'pause' in our friendship there was never a 'break.' My *Belleville Telescope* editorials opposing the *Bull Moose* movement were carried on page one, column one of the *Kansas City Journal.* Roosevelt carried Kansas but George Hodges, the Democratic candidate for governor, defeated Capper by 29 votes. Capper accepted his defeat without rancor, and despite the closeness of the race, refused to ask for a recount of the votes.

"Two years later Capper got the Republican nomination for governor again and was elected. When I found out that Capper was to run again I wrote to Charlie Sessions, editor of the *Capital,* and suggested that the candidate open the campaign at Belleville, in April. Sessions thought this was a little too early but he agreed. The Belleville court house had an overflow crowd when I introduced Capper. At this time he read his speech but he was to become a very impressive campaign speaker and soon gave up the practice of reading his speeches. As evidence of the fact that Capper bore no grudge for our differences of political opinion in 1912, after he was elected governor, he appointed me chairman of the State Board of Corrections in charge of the state's penal institutions.

"In public life, as Governor and later United States Senator, Capper's basic principle was that he was a servant of the people not their master. Upon important national questions he tried to find out the sentiment of his constituents and endeavored, as far as possible, with his fuller vantage point in Washington to represent them. The 4,000,000 readers of his farm publications put him in an unusual position in regard to obtaining public sentiment on any question. In Washington he was regarded as an authority on agriculture and his impress was stamped on much farm legislation.

"His personal life and political integrity were never questioned, even by his opponents.

"H. S. Blake, vice-president and general manager of the Capper Publications, paid the following tribute to Senator Capper: 'A kinder and gentler man never lived; he never knowingly hurt anyone. We did not work for Arthur Capper — we worked with him. Never in the 32 years I worked with him did a harsh word ever pass his lips, no matter how troubled the times; never once in all the years I knew him did he ever use a swear word or tell an off-color story; he never asked an employee's religion or political affiliation.'

"President Truman wired: 'It may almost be said that an era in the history of the old Mid-West came to a close with the passing of Senator Capper.' Roy Roberts, editor of the *Kansas City Star,* said: 'Instinctively Arthur Capper liked people, especially children; it did not make any difference whether the person was high or low, Capper would strike up a conversation. He was definitely a friend of the common man."

Merle Thorpe — Teacher, Editor, Business Executive

"Merle Thorpe, former Dean of Journalism at Kansas University, is another Kansas journalist who made good in a big way. A firm believer in free enterprise, resourceful and indefatigable, Thorpe was bound to succeed in any endeavor toward which he directed his talents.

"At the turn of the century Thorpe was teaching journalism at Kansas University. Together with Charles M. Harger, editor of the *Abilene Reflector* and member of the State Board of Regents, he organized the School of Journalism at K.U. and served as its Dean.

"On May 10, 1914, when the Kansas Editorial Association met at Lawrence, Merle Thorpe announced a program that obtained widespread publicity throughout the nation for its novelty and its soundness. He had persuaded all the ministers in Lawrence to vacate their pulpits on the morning and evening of the Sunday preceding the Editorial Association's meeting and detailed various Kansas editors to deliver "lay-sermons" from the Lawrence pulpits. Fourteen Kansas editors addressed the congregations on 'The Press and the Pulpit.' Here is the list of the speakers:

William Allen White, *Emporia Gazette;* Charles Moreau Harger, *Abilene Reflector;* E. E. Kelley, *Toronto Republican;* B. J. Sheridan, *Paola Western Spirit;* Henry J. Allen, *Wichita Beacon;* Homer Hoch, *Marion Record;* Ewing Herbert, *Brown County World;* A. Q. Miller, *Belleville Telescope;* W. Y. Morgan, *Hutchinson News;* George Marble, *Fort Scott Tribune; Arthur Capper,* Capper Publications; Imri Zumwalt, *Bonner Springs Chieftain;* W. E. Miller, *St. Mary's Star;* F. W. Knapp, *Beloit Gazette.*

"Noting the outstanding work of Merle Thorpe at K.U. the *Nation's Business,* outstanding business publication, secured his

Merle Thorpe, a Kansas journalist who achieved national fame as editor of THE NATION'S BUSINESS. *Formerly chairman of the Journalism Department at Kansas University, Thorpe was an inspiration to his hundreds of students. A. Q. Miller's son Merle is named after him.*

services as manager. From a circulation of 30,000 when he assumed his office, *Nation's Business* grew to over half a million in two decades.

"Recognizing Thorpe's outstanding ability as an executive and an administrator, the Cities Service Company named him a member of its executive board in New York. It has become almost a tradition for great industries, who want new blood in their organizations, to select men from the middle west.

"On May 22, 1946, a special meeting of the Kansas University Alumni Association was held at Lawrence. Professor L. N. Flint was guest of honor at a dinner marking his retirement from active service as Dean of Journalism. Elmer F. Beth, acting chairman of the *University Daily Kansan* Board, invited Merle Thorpe to deliver the principal address. In searching for an old friend of Thorpe's to introduce him as the guest speaker, Mr. Beth conferred this honor on me.

"Almost forty-five years before the date of the above mentioned meeting and while he was still head of K.U.'s journalism department, Merle Thorpe was a guest at my home in Belleville. We got on the subject of journalism and the discussion carried us far into the night. I was completely carried away with Merle Thorpe's enthusiasm and the picture he painted for the future of journalism. I later named my son, Merle, for this distinguished journalist, who has always been a credit to his profession and his native Kansas."

Colonel W. R. Nelson and the Kansas City Star

"The *Kansas City Star* is one of the greatest newspapers in the United States. Under the management of the late Colonel W. R. Nelson the *Star* became more than a great newspaper. For Kansas City and much of Kansas the *Star* was an institution. It used its power for civic improvements where Nelson wanted them; it threw its influence behind political candidates, local, state and national, whose views happened to coincide with those of Nelson. Under the administration of President Grover Cleveland the *Star* was a "low tariff" newspaper; it supported both Teddy and Franklin Roosevelt in their campaigns for the presidency. When Teddy Roosevelt organized the Bull Moose party, the Star was right behind him.

"Following the death of the colorful Colonel Nelson the *Star* has pursued a more conservative and independent course. One of its greatest crusades was the exposure of the Pendergast political machine in Kansas City. This resulted in the rout of the organization which had dominated Kansas City for so many years. The political "boss" wound up in the penitentiary.

"The *Kansas City Star,* throughout all the years, has been an extremely courageous newspaper. Fighting bitter battles on many fronts made the *Star* many enemies and for years a half dozen daily newspapers sought "unsuccessfully" to put it out of business.

"I first became acquainted with Colonel W. R. Nelson during the 1890's. I visited Kansas City frequently, traveling on railroad passes which were issued to newspapers in exchange for advertising. I called at the *Star* office on the corner of 11th St. and Grand Avenue and remember, vividly, Colonel Nelson, in his shirt sleeves, sitting behind a flat top desk in the corner of the editorial room.

"That was in the days of horse-drawn street cars and the Ninth Street incline cable car which brought passenger traffic up a 23 per cent grade from the Union Station to Kansas City's business section. Across the street from the Union Depot was the Blossom House, political headquarters for Kansas. This was exceeded in importance only by the Copeland Hotel in Topeka. For approximately thirty years, candidates were made or broken in caucuses at one or the other of these two historic hotels.

"This was during the day of Cy Leland, Mort Albaugh,

George A. Clark, Walter Roscoe Stubbs, William A. Peffer, "Sockless" Jerry Simpson, Mary Ellen Lease and John W. Leedy. It was during the time when J. R. Burton of Abilene was trying to unseat Senator John R. Ingalls of Atchison. During these years there were no political conventions, as such. Candidates for office were picked by and with the consent of party leaders. This was before Walter Roscoe Stubbs, a railroad contractor, crashed into the State House as governor. Stubbs wrote the primary election law; sponsored bills destroying political railroad passes and enacted many other reform measures.

"Colonel Nelson and the *Kansas City Star* had become a power in Missouri, Kansas and national politics.

"Ed Hoch, editor of the *Marion Record,* while serving as a member of the State Legislature had displayed a great deal of political independence and incurred the displeasure of the *Star.* He became a candidate for the office of State Printer, which in those days was elected by the legislature. Hoch refused to make any political deals and a combination of legislators blocked his election. When the final vote was counted at a midnight session of the legislature Hoch was defeated. Called on for a statement Hoch said: 'Gentlemen, I came out of this fight with empty hands but thank God they are clean ones.'

"The aftermath of the bitter fight in the legislature, during the election for State Printer, resulted in Hoch's being nominated for governor. Despite the fact that he was actively opposed by the *Kansas City Star,* Hoch was elected. There is no doubt that Hoch's election was the result of a growing feeling that the *Star* was exercising too much influence on the Kansas political scene.

"During his campaign for governor Ed Hoch spoke to a capacity crowd at the Court House in Belleville. He delivered one of his characteristic and effective speeches. I wired the story of the meeting to the *Star.* The story that appeared in the *Star* bore not the slightest resemblance to my dispatch, obviously it had been re-written in the *Star's* editorial room. In the very next issue of the *Belleville Telescope,* I wrote a highly critical editorial on the *Star's* political ethics. Among other comments I remarked: 'It is time to move the Kansas Capital from the editorial rooms of the *Kansas City Star* back to Topeka where it belongs.' This phrase proved popular with critics of the *Star* and was often used by them.

"The net result of my campaign against the *Star* was that my exchange copy of the *Star* was discontinued and my contract as a correspondent was cancelled. Incensed, I decided to 'put the *Star* out of business.' For the next few years I worked steadily toward this objective. My father, who was living in Kansas City, used to stroll down to the *Star* office and from there write me a letter saying that the *Star* was still there. I finally decided to abandon this objective, since my campaign did not seem to be paralyzing the *Star's* activities.

"Agree with them or not, Colonel W. R. Nelson and the *Kansas City Star* were two of Kansas' outstanding institutions for a good many years and one looks back at their heyday with just a bit of fond nostalgia."

Henry J. Allen — Journalist, Statesman

"Henry J. Allen, journalist, governor and United States Senator, was a top flight political leader in state and national affairs for half a century.

"Born on a farm near Cory, Pa., Sept. 12, 1878, he was brought to Kansas by his parents when he was five. He attended Baker University at Baldwin but left school in 1891 to become a cub reporter on the *Salina Republican.*

"In 1894, Allen bought the *Manhattan Nationalist* and edited it for two years. He then joined his former *Salina Republican* boss, Senator Joseph Bristow, in ownership and publication

The late Henry J. Allen, Kansas journalist, former Governor of Kansas and United States Senator.

of the *Ottawa Herald,* a weekly. They changed the *Herald* to a daily, then joined in purchasing and combining two Salina newspapers as the *Evening Journal.*

"When Bristow retired, the two men divided their property, Allen getting the *Herald* and Bristow the *Journal.* Allen purchased the *Parsons Daily Sun, Fort Scott Republican* and a Garden City weekly which he changed to a daily, the *Evening Telegram.*

"He sold the *Ottawa Herald* in 1907 to R. A. Harris, father of the present owners and publishers. He sold the *Parsons Sun* to the late Clyde M. Reed and sold his other two newspapers, closing out all other interests to concentrate on the *Wichita Beacon.*

"He immediately started a campaign against the open saloons that were running in defiance of Kansas' prohibition law and, with the support of H. H. Motter, Internal Revenue Collector, and Rev. John McFadden, Methodist pastor, drove them out.

"Allen was known all over the state for his oratorical ability and was a leading speaker at debates scheduled by the Redpath-Horner Chautauqua bureau. Allen, who had bolted the Republican party in 1912, with Teddy Roosevelt engaged in some stormy verbal battles in his support of the 'Bull-Moose' movement. In 1914 he ran for governor on the third party ticket, finishing a poor third. By 1916 he was back in the Republican fold.

"When Senator Charles Curtis was elected vice-president with Herbert Hoover his senatorial seat was left vacant. Kansas' governor, Clyde Reed, appointed Henry Allen to fill the vacancy. Allen had been a staunch supporter of Hoover and helped in the handling of his public relations. He played a courageous role on the floor during the hectic years of Hoover's administration.

"Hoover, a much misrepresented and maligned man, was not a popular president. The average Republican was afraid to actively support his measures for fear of censure. Senator Allen joined forces with the Republican floor leader, Senator Jim

Watson of Indiana, in helping to support President Hoover's measures. Many fearful Republicans remained absent from the floor when legislation was being voted on.

"Contrary to the custom of the Senate which held that new members or freshmen, as they were called, must be seen and not heard, Senator Allen repeatedly took the floor. He was hazed and asked embarrassing questions repeatedly by the opposition solons. A seasoned orator and debater, Allen stood his ground and took them on in twos and threes until they decided they had best leave the freshman from Kansas alone.

"In 1932, Allen ran for the full senatorial term and asked me to handle his primary petitions and publicity. Allen's opponent was George McGill, a Wichita lawyer with only a local reputation. Few Democrats were willing to challenge Allen for the seat in the Senate. Allen depended on his state-wide acquaintance, experience as a legislator and other qualifications for the office. This was not enough. McGill covered every corner of the state in a Model T Ford. He spoke at small cross roads and shook hands with farmers, factory workers and day laborers. When the returns were in McGill, along with a vast majority of 1932 Democrats, was victor by a small margin.

"Allen, like his good friend Bill White, of Emporia, never carried a political grudge and remained popular with both political factions in the state. During World War I he was active in Y.M.C.A. activities and served abroad. He helped establish the American Red Cross Home Communication System—which helped keep soldiers in touch with the folks at home.

"During World War II he was a leader in the 'Bundles for Britain' and 'Save the Children Foundation' projects. For his outstanding efforts he was decorated, in 1946, by King George VI.

"When Henry Allen died at his home in Wichita at the age of 81, Kansas and the entire nation mourned the passing of an outstanding citizen."

William Allen White — Country Editor

"No Kansan ever attained a wider acquaintance than William Allen White, editor and publisher of the *Emporia Gazette.* He achieved national prominence as the 'Sage of Emporia' and was certainly one of Kansas' most unique and colorful citizens. Through his books, articles and editorials he achieved an international reputation. He was entertained by the nobility of many foreign nations and was the confidante of half a dozen American presidents. He became a prominent figure in the political life of the nation and was generally credited with accurately interpreting Kansas thinking. Across half a century of tempestuous political years, William Allen White embraced many reform movements. During this time I was accused of being an 'unregenerated stand-patter.'

"Though we differed widely in our political philosophy, only on occasion finding common ground for agreement, we remained personal friends for over fifty years. His autographed picture hangs over my desk and my files contained hundreds of his letters on personal and political subjects.

"In 1895, Bill White borrowed $3,000 and bought the *Emporia Gazette.* He was a country editor then and from that day on prided himself on that title. He turned down countless opportunities to associate himself with nationally known metropolitan newspapers. He told those who wanted him to leave Emporia for greater things: 'If you like neighbors and neighboring — which means kindly relations with folks deeply rooted in your life — then leave the great city.'

"White was always accused of being inconsistent in his political thinking. His reply was: 'Some of my best friends of a lifetime differed from me violently in my political philosophy but there was something deeper and finer in that friendship which bound us together.'

"On two distinct occasions the political differences between Bill White and myself were very wide. The first was when William Allen White joined the 'Bull Moose' party when this group was organized by Teddy Roosevelt, Senator Hiram Johnson, of California, Harold Ickes, W. R. Nelson, of the *Kansas City Star,* Senators Arthur Capper and Henry Allen and Governor Walter R. Stubbs, of Kansas.

"I was a sergeant-at-arms at the Chicago National Republican Convention of 1912 which nominated William Howard Taft. This nomination resulted in the formation of the third party which Chicago newspapers, at the time, said was a religious movement hence morally all right to be formed on a Sunday.

"During the convention I read every issue of all the Chicago newspapers reporting the convention and, of course, followed the procedure on the convention floor. It was my opinion that the so called 'stolen nomination' for Taft was a political stunt designed to alienate the people of the nation against the candidate. From my vantage point I could see nothing irregular in the formation and procedure of the convention. I believed then, and still do, that the real cause of the split in the Republican party was due to a disagreement between Taft and Roosevelt.

"Colonel Roosevelt had helped secure the nomination of Taft for the first term as his successor. Roosevelt then went to Africa on a big game hunt. President Taft, of judicial temperament and conviction did not believe in some of the measures advocated by Roosevelt, when he was president, and his first term was a conservative one. This displeased the Rough Rider. Since he could not persuade Taft to abandon his conservative policies and could not win the nomination for himself, Roosevelt organized the Bull Moose party on that long ago Sunday morning. What started as a protest against President Taft served to elect the Democrat, Woodrow Wilson, to the presidency.

"Many leaders of the Republican party, as well as innumerable

An excellent character study of Kansas beloved William Allen White. Known far and wide as the Sage of Emporia, White's editorials were avidly read by millions in this country and abroad.

metropolitan newspapers, joined the movement with Roosevelt. There is no doubt that this wide split in the Republican party contributed to the successful campaign of Woodrow Wilson. Personally I stuck to my convictions about the nomination and wrote the convention story as I saw it:

" 'On account of the wide publicity and volume of propaganda that has gone out about the Chicago Convention, I realize that readers of the *Belleville Telescope* will not be in a frame of mind to accept my version of the convention happenings. Nevertheless, true to my convictions, I am going to give my version of what happened at Chicago.'

"After composing this lead paragraph, I walked the floor until about two o'clock in the morning. I was convinced that my readers would not believe my story.

" 'There was a contested delegation from California. This was brought about by an unofficial roll call by California's Senator Hiram Johnson. The delegation had not been legally seated by the credential committee. Despite this Senator Johnson stood on his seat in the convention hall and tried repeatedly to vote the delegation for Roosevelt.'

"I went on to explain that this was just one aspect of the convention but that in my mind there was nothing illegal about the nomination and that President William Howard Taft was the real Republican candidate and therefore deserved the support of his party.

"The Bull-Moosers conducted an aggressive campaign. From a chartered train which moved across the nation Roosevelt spoke at every 'whistle stop.' When the train stopped at Manhattan, Kansas, I was invited to join the official welcoming party, as a newspaper editor.

"After Roosevelt had made his speech from the platform of the observation car he returned to the interior and was complimented and greeted by a large number of Topeka politicians and correspondents. Teddy spied Governor Stubbs and they greeted each other in a spontaneous bear hug. This was the first time they had met since the Chicago Convention. I was standing only a few feet away and heard Roosevelt tell Stubbs: 'He (Taft) is in our way; we've got to knock him out.' A 'stand-pat Republican,' this didn't set too well with me and I turned and got off the train before being introduced to the redoubtable 'Teddy.'

"My next major political difference with Bill White occurred in the fall of 1941. White had attacked the entire Kansas congressional delegation editorially: 'I am going to see that a new set of Congressmen is put up in the primaries and get some new faces in Washington, representatives that will support President Roosevelt in his foreign policy.'

"The *Kansas City Star* printed many of the White editorials on the first page and they were quoted liberally in a subsequent campaign by the Roosevelt advocates. Editorially I took issue with Mr. White, pointing out the warnings of Washington and Jefferson against entangling foreign alliances. I also stated that congressmen are elected by the people to represent their districts and are accountable to their constituents — not the President.

"As in the days of my feud with the *Kansas City Star* I took my little slingshot, and with considerable temerity, set out to slay the giant of Cottonwood valley. My first letter to Bill White, marked personal, was dated December 5, 1941, and opened, 'My dear friend: It is with considerable trepidation that I write this personal note to you, but I feel the importance of the issues involved in your editorial comments so keenly that I must do it at the risk of breeching a life-long friendship.' I followed this with a lay sermon from me as an amateur politician beseeching White not to carry out his threat to put another full congressional ticket in the Republican primary. I pointed out that most of these representatives were voicing the feeling of their constituents who were critical of the President's foreign policy and in my opinion they should be re-elected.

"While I don't think my letter was a major factor in the change of heart, the temperature around Emporia cooled off and White did not put up a new slate of congressional candidates in the primaries. In fact he supported and helped re-elect all the incumbents. I particularly value the answer to my letter received from Bill White:

" 'Dear A. Q.: Don't ever approach me with considerable trepidation; we have been country editors too long for you to get any notions that I can't take a frank expression of a difference of opinion from an old friend. I have said over and over again that these congressmen have a right to say and do what they please, but their constituents have a Royal American right to vote and act as they please; that's what I am doing; we are going to take the matter into the Republican primary and make it a Republican fight; that's what we did when Senator Chester Long got out of step. I hope this explains my position. Sincerely, W. A. White.'

"One of William Allen White's outstanding characteristics was his human impulse and emotion and his skill at inventing expressive phrases. I would like to quote a typical example from a letter in my personal file:

"(March 24, 1943) 'We are in a devil of a fix; when there is a bully in the school yard no boy is safe until all the boys lick him; the same is true of this world, that has been shrunken by airplane and radio; we will have only as much freedom as we guarantee others.'

"Bill White never sought, and would not accept, public office. He maintained that, as a country editor, he wanted to be free to criticize or praise a public official or political party. There was one exception to this, however. He became candidate for governor on an independent ticket, as a protest against the candidacy of Dr. Brinkley and the growth of the Ku Klux Klan. Tolerance was one of the cornerstones of White's personal faith and he believed his candidacy would give him a greater opportunity to expose the activities of the Klan in Kansas. He received a substantial vote in the election.

"William Allen White's wife joined her husband in entertaining their many friends. Those who have been beneficiaries of their hospitality can attest to Mrs. White's culinary abilities and personal charm as a hostess. I well recall one occasion when Bill had just returned from a trip to Russia and other European countries. I was in a group of editors he invited to his home for dinner and to hear about his trip. After a delicious meal we adjourned to the parlor and sprawled comfortably about the room. White sat on a bear skin rug in front of the fireplace and told about his trip, answering questions as he went along. I don't know when I ever spent a more memorable evening.

"In the middle of the *Gazette's* editorial office was an old fashioned roll top desk that was almost as famous as its occupant. It had been in hundreds of pictures of the 'Sage of Emporia'; piled high with miscellaneous clippings, newspaprs, letters, etc. It had many pigeon holes for filing and these were jam packed. One day, calling at the *Gazette* office, I asked White if the papers on his desk, were the same ones that had been there on my previous visit a year before. He replied that he thought they were.

"This roll top desk was something of a country editor's trade mark. I recall the desk that used to be in the office of the *Belleville Telescope.* I bought it second hand from banker in 1906 for $10. It had 46 pigeon holes which served as my filing system for many years. Later when my sons took over active editorship of the *Telescope* they installed a modern filing and bookkeeping system and somewhat hesitantly asked me if they could move the old relic out of the office. I could not stand in the way of progress.

William Allen White, shown at his desk in Emporia. This crowded roll top became White's trade mark during his career as the nation's most outstanding country editor.

"One of my favorite stories about William Allen White, is true, and concerns Walt Mason, nationally-known writer and poet. Walt had worked on a newspaper in Beatrice, Nebraska. He had an exceptional talent for writing poetry and everything rolled from his pencil in the form of a jingle. Mason, however, had a weakness for the demon rum and twice took the cure at Kansas City's Keeley Institute. After his second graduation from this institution he drifted to Topeka where he knew and was known to many of the newspaper crowd. The Topeka newsmen decided to play a good joke on William Allen White and they passed the hat, raised money for Mason's transportation to Emporia. They wired White, told him Mason was en route and suggested that Bill give him a job.

"White hired Mason and Walt proceeded to write up all the local news in jingle style. The technique proved popular and a national syndicate became interested in Mason's work. They asked him to write a column for syndication and sold it all over the nation. Walt Mason soon became a wealthy man and retired to California. I was visiting White shortly after Mason became a syndicated writer and Bill told me that the man sent to him for a gag was making more money than he was.

"Bill White had a wonderful sense of humor and could make a commonplace occurrence an excuse for laugh producing prose. I had not been on the exchange list with the *Gazette* and mentioned this to White who promised to look into the matter. After a while he wrote me: 'I have tried to get the circulation department to place your name on the complimentary exchange list, but you know the circulation department of every newspaper has registered a mighty vow, written in blood, never to put a subscriber on the list who is friend of the editor. Forty-five long years I have been connected with newspapers as mailing boy, city circulator, reporter, advertising solicitor, business manager, editorial writer and manager and I have never known that rule to fail. In due course when the slow grinding gods of the circulation department get you through the mill, you will get on; at least that is my pious prayer.'

"Many books have already been written about the 'Sage of Emporia' who has become a journalistic legend. Many more could be written, and probably will be. I can't think of any man who exercised such a benign influence over such a great area as William Allen White did from behind that old roll top desk in Emporia. These few hap-hazard recollections will serve, in a small way, to give readers an insight into the personality of this great man whose friendship I was privileged to share during the greater part of our lives."

Guy Helvering and Harry Woodring, Bankers and Statesmen

"It is interesting to recall how a minor meeting of these two gentlemen determined their future to such a large degree. Guy Helvering happened to be in his bank at Salina, Kansas, on a certain day in June of 1930. Word was sent into this office that another banker from Neodesha, Kansas, was waiting to see him. The outcome of this seemingly routine happening resulted in Harry Woodring being appointed Assistant Secretary of War and Mr. Helvering being named as Commissioner of Internal Revenue.

"During my lifetime I have never failed to be impressed by how often political fortunes hinge on just such commonplace events.

"At the time of the meeting, mentioned above, Guy Helvering had definitely retired from politics. He had served the old fifth district in the national Congress and having done his stint was devoting his time to his banking business. Harry Woodring, also a banker, was practically unknown in state political circles.

Woodring was interested in obtaining the primary nomination for governor, on the Democratic ticket, and wanted Helvering to help him obtain a few votes.

"Helvering told me later that he had absolutely no intention of going back into politics but he was so impressed with the personality, frankness and apparent ability of the Neodesha banker that he decided to abandon his previous resolution. Helvering and Woodring drove to Marysville and had a conference with Lynn Broderick, National Democratic Committeeman. After this the campaign was on. That summer Helvering, once again, left his bank and, with Woodring, drove all over northern Kansas. Former Congressman Helvering was well known to thousands of voters in this area.

"Harry Woodring was nominated in the Democratic primary by a safe margin. This victory automatically made Helvering state chairman and he conducted a vigorous campaign to elect the man of his choice. A slender margin of 242 votes resulted in Woodring and Helvering continuing in politics instead of returning to their banking businesses. Upon Woodring's election as governor, Helvering was appointed to the important post of highway director.

"The friendship of these two men was a continuing one. Furthermore they saw eye to eye on most political issues. A notable example of their political affinity was their championing of Franklin D. Roosevelt for the Democratic presidential nomination over Alfred E. Smith. At the time of the Democratic national convention in Chicago, Kansas sentiment seemed to favor former New York governor, Alfred E. Smith. Woodring and Helvering, however, were impressed with the progressive ideas and popularity of New York's governor, Franklin D. Roosevelt. They made several pre-convention trips to Albany to discuss affairs with Governor Roosevelt. Helvering and

Woodring were on the Democratic delegation to the Chicago convention. When the contest was over and the smoke had cleared away, Roosevelt was nominated for president and he received the votes of Kansas' delegation, thanks to his two supporters, Woodring and Helvering.

"In the presidential election of 1932, Roosevelt swept Kansas but Woodring, running on the Democratic ticket for re-election as governor, was defeated. This again confirmed the Kansas precedent that no Democratic governor was ever re-elected for a second term. Despite his defeat for governor, Woodring and Helvering were in a strategic position in Kansas and national politics. They had already won the confidence of James Farley, Democratic national chairman and an extremely astute politician. Having Farley's support was no liability in the early years of the Roosevelt administration.

"Another paradox had occurred in Kansas politics. George McGill, a Wichita attorney, was swept into office as United States Senator. McGill, without any support or endorsement from the state committee, had conducted a very effective grass roots campaign from the running board of his automobile. He was elected without being under obligation to any political group. His election created a complex problem regarding federal patronage in Kansas. McGill, in the Senate, had the authority to confirm or reject Kansas federal appointments. Helvering and Woodring did not see eye to eye with the new Senator regarding these appointments. President Roosevelt did not want to make an issue of this controversy, so a working agreement was reached on the Kansas appointments.

"Shortly after this Harry Woodring was appointed assistant Secretary of War. Guy Helvering, later, was appointed Commissioner of Internal Revenue, a position equal in importance to a place on the cabinet. Both Woodring and Helvering served their country well as federal appointees. They had the respect and friendship of their party. Both James Farley, on the national scene, and Lynn Broderick, in Kansas gave their continuing support to the two Kansans who had risen to national prominence as a result of their meeting in Salina in June of 1930 and a 242 vote majority in the Kansas gubernatorial campaign."

Editor's Note — Although Mr. A. Q. Miller, Sr., continually refers to himself as a "stand-pat" Republican it is plain to any observer, from his remarks on Harry Woodring and Guy Helvering, that his admiration for many fellow Kansans easily transcended his Republicanism. Typical of his support of ethical men in public office, regardless of their political affiliation, is the following editorial. Mr. Miller wrote this for the March 15, 1934 issue of the *Belleville Telescope* when Harry Woodring was "under-fire" in Washington.

"HARRY WOODRING AND AIRPLANE CONTRACTS

"The Kansas friends of Harry H. Woodring, assistant Secretary of War, never lost confidence in Kansas' former governor during the airplane sale investigation in Washington.

"While early reports cast a cloud of suspicion upon the policy used in purchase of planes for the government, none who knew Harry Woodring, either as a banker at Neodesha or as governor of Kansas, believed the investigation would touch him personally or officially — that he would be in any wise connected with improper conduct in government negotiations for army planes.

"As the evidence and facts were unfolded it was disclosed that it was Mr. Woodring who broke up the established policy of selling army planes to the government on the basis of 'negotiation' or 'cost plus' without competitive bids. It was the assistant Secretary of War who insisted that competitive bids should be received in the new expenditure of $7,500,000 for army planes.

"It is easy to understand the disappointment and consternation in the ranks of manufacturers of airplanes who had been successful 'negotiators' in selling their planes to the government on the 'cost plus' basis. They would under the New Deal, be required to put their cards on top of the table.

"It is easy to understand why they would resent such interference from a 'freshman' who came out of the West — from Kansas. It is easy to understand why the wolves would howl and try to devour the assistant Secretary of War — but he stood adamant and was not afraid of the 'big bad wolf.'

"There is nothing unusual about attorneys or lobbyists appearing in Washington in behalf of special interests. This practice has been followed from time immemorial. The important thing is that such influence did not touch Mr. Woodring or deter him from his original purpose; to receive competitive bids in awarding airplane contracts.

"The assistant Secretary of War, from Kansas, came through the investigation untouched and fully exonerated in the eyes of public opinion because he stood four square on a policy of handling public business. To Mr. Woodring will go the credit for breaking up a reprehensible practice in awarding government contracts."

Edwin C. Johnson, Statesman, United States Senator

"Senator Edwin C. Johnson was born five miles west of Belleville. His birthplace is located just off what is known as U. S. Highway 36. Primarily a self-made man, Johnson has been the architect of his own career. His achievements are an example and an inspiration to his colleagues and the youth of the nation.

"Graduated from Lincoln High School in 1903, Johnson worked as laborer on the railroad and rose successively to telegrapher and train dispatcher. He later became a homesteader and

Edwin C. Johnson, former United States Senator, now Governor of Colorado. A lifelong friend of A. Q. Miller.

manager of a farmers cooperative association. A Democrat, he was elected to the Colorado Legislature for four successive terms, from 1923 to 1931. He served as Lt. Governor of Colorado for two terms. He has twice been Governor of Colorado. From this office he was elected to the United States Senate.

"While serving as Governor of Colorado, in the 1930's, Johnson allotted the lion's share of Colorado's federal work funds to the improvement of U. S. 36 from Denver to the Kansas line. Bridges and culverts were constructed and a standard grade was established. Johnson maintained that improvement of U. S. 36 was important to the welfare of the state. Colorado was being by-passed by many tourists because the more improved highways were routed around Colorado.

"As United States Senator from Colorado Johnson was not a strict 'party-line' follower. During the Roosevelt and Truman administrations he did not hesitate to take the floor and vigorously oppose New Deal measures which he believed were not in the best interests of the nation. An example of his feeling concerning certain legislation is to be found in a letter he wrote me in November of 1945 about an editorial in the *Belleville Telescope:*

" 'I am glad to have your reactions to the President's military training bill; the scheme is Prussianism and nothing else; I'm opposed to this venture into militarism and shall fight it to the last ditch.' Continuing the Senator said: 'Whole heartedly I join in insisting upon military security for our country, but strange as it may seem, military security in the atomic age will be found in the school room and not in the boot camp. I am very grateful to you for the assistance which you are giving me in the fight against peacetime conscription.'

"Ed Johnson's life is another example of America's being the land of opportunity. From section hand to senior senator is a long step for any man. But Ed Johnson knows the same people now that he did when he first appeared in the State House in Colorado as an unknown member of the legislature from the Western Slope. He made no effort to attract attention, just plugged along with his job. After a while the smart men around the State House began to mention that the big Swede from the Western Slope was a pretty able man.

"In his various campaigns for office he became widely known and it has been said of him that he can walk into any court house in the 63 counties of Colorado and call most of the officials by their first name. And to most people who know him he is Ed Johnson.

"Ed Johnson was always popular with his constituents. He never hesitated to take a stand on a controversial question. Regardless of political distinction, Johnson stood for what he contended was the best interest of the country."

Palmer Hoyt, Publisher

Although not a Kansan, Palmer Hoyt has always been a friend of Kansas. Through the *Denver Post* he did much to speed improvements on U. S. 36. He has been a close friend of A. Q. Miller for many years.

Before his appointment in February, 1946, as editor and publisher of the *Denver Post,* Palmer Hoyt had in 13 years risen from copy desk man to publisher of *The Oregonian,* the outstanding morning newspaper of Portland, Oregon.

Upon graduation from the University of Oregon's school of journalism in 1923, Palmer Hoyt spent a brief two months at *The Oregonian* before going to the Pendleton *East Oregonian* for a three-year term as telegraph editor. In 1926 he returned to *The Oregonian* as a copy editor.

In 1928 he started general reporting. The next year he became drama editor, and in 1930 was made night city editor. Promo-

Palmer Hoyt, publisher of the nationally known Denver Post, a famous journalist and a many year friend of A. Q. Miller, Sr., and the Sunflower State.

tion to the post of executive news editor occurred on August 1, 1931. In just two years Hoyt was appointed managing editor of the paper.

Recognition for his earlier successes came in February, 1939, when Palmer Hoyt was given the paper's top position of responsibility as publisher. This followed by only five months his appointment as *The Oregonian's* general manager.

Hoyt's public service was not confined to his position on *The Oregonian.* He was elected national president of Sigma Delta Chi, honorary journalism fraternity, for the year 1942-3-. At a time when the treatment of war news posed a vital problem for the nation's welfare, Hoyt served his nation as domestic director of the Office of War Information. Later, official recognition was to be his again after coming to the *Denver Post,* when from July, 1947, to January, 1948, he was to serve as a member of the President's Air Policy Commission in framing recommendations for the national defense.

Other posts held by Hoyt have included chairmanship of the War Bond Committee of Oregon from 1941 to 1943 and the presidency of the Oregon Newspaper Publishers association, 1943 to 1945. He is also a director of the Associated Press. After coming to Denver, he was named chairman of the Denver Area Community Chest drive in 1948, and president of the Denver Community Chest in 1949, and again in 1950.

Hoyt's work as a newspaperman has not been confined to the filling of official posts, for he has written and sold more than 50 short stories.

And, as a citizen, he served not only in World War II in the capacity mentioned, but in World War I he was with the infantry. He enlisted in March, 1917, with Company A, Third Oregon infantry, which was later the 162nd infantry. After service of 18 months in France, he was discharged with the rank of sergeant major.

In addition to Sigma Delta Chi, he is also a member of Chi Psi fraternity, Sigma Upsilon, Rotary, Denver Club, and Denver Athletic club. He was born March 10, 1897, in Roseville, Illinois, son of (Edwin) Palmer Hoyt, Baptist minister, and Annie (Tendler) Hoyt. In 1921 he married Cecile DeVore. They reared two sons, Edwin Palmer Hoyt and Charles Richard Hoyt. They were divorced in 1950. In November, 1950, Palmer Hoyt married Helen May Taber. They have a son, Lincoln Porter Hoyt.

Before enrolling at the University of Oregon in 1919, Hoyt attended prep school at William Jewell college in Liberty, Missouri, and McMinnville College (now Linfield) in Oregon.

Albert T. Reid, Cartoonist, Artist, Lecturer

"One of my prized friendships, which reaches back more than sixty years, is that of Albert T. Reid, internationally-famous artist and cartoonist. Reid was born in Concordia, Kansas, and attended school in Clyde. He was a printer's devil on the *Clyde Argus* at the time I held the same exalted position on the *Clifton News.* We became boyhood friends and have remained so all these years.

"I recall vividly the thrill I got when I saw a prize winning cartoon by Albert Reid on the first page of the *Topeka Mail and Breeze.* The weekly cartoons which then began to appear in the *Mail & Breeze* started the amateur cartoonist on the road to fame — by way of the *Kansas City Star.*

"In Reid's school days, he told me, he was so interested in art and printing that he was anything but a prize student. On one occasion his mother checked up with his teacher on Al's school attendance. The teacher hardly knew him. He was so busy drawing pictures in the text books of his student friends and painting on barn doors and outbuildings in Clyde that his school attendance and marks began to suffer.

Coronado visits Kansas, famous painting by Albert T. Reid, depicts famed conquistadore's early appearance on the Kansas scene.

"After graduation from high school Reid became an expert typesetter or compositor on the *Argus.* The editor of the paper decided that Reid was competent enough that he could take a week off from his editorial duties. So the young printer was left with the entire responsibility of getting out the paper. Everything went along fine until it was discovered that the 'boiler plate,' or stock printing matter, was being held C.O.D. at the Post Office. Reid didn't have nearly enough money to get the material out of hock. Clyde merchants hearing of his dilemma took up a collection for Reid so that he could redeem the boiler plate and the paper came out on time.

"About a year after Reid began to be published in the *Topeka Mail and Breeze* he was hired by the *Kansas City Star.* From the *Star,* Reid went to the magazine *Judge* and then to the *New York Herald* as art director. In 1919, Reid a longtime friend of Republican politicians was summoned to New York to handle Republican pictorial publicity. When someone suggested that more people would use the pictorial material if it were under Reid's name, he formed his own syndicate.

"He continued to produce cartoons for his own syndicate while engaged in illustrating fiction for some of the nation's leading magazines. For many years he was associated with Hearst columnist, Arthur Brisbane. Every issue of the Hearst Sunday paper carried a large Reid cartoon with a Brisbane editorial beneath it.

"Reid's political cartoons had an important influence on the big issues of the day. The late Senator Henry Cabot Lodge of Massachusetts called Reid's cartoon *Article Ten Wants Your Boy* the most powerful and effective political cartoon ever drawn. This cartoon was instrumental in helping direct public opinion against U. S. entry into the League of Nations.

"In 1936, Reid stopped cartooning but his interest in politics never diminished. According to the famous artist, 'if you're born in Kansas you matriculate in politics.' In 1952 he again served the Republicans on the *Artists For Eisenhower Committee.*

"Reid, remembering his struggle for recognition, has been extremely helpful to his fellow artists. Quite a few years ago the *Belleville Telescope* began publishing cartoons by a Belleville boy. These attracted the attention of the *Kansas City Star* and I selected a portfolio of the young man's works and sent them to Mr. A. Wood, the *Star's* art director. The *Star* hired the young man. Before Jefferson Machamer, now a nationally-famous cartoonist, went to Kansas Ctiy, I arranged a meeting for him with Albert Reid who was visiting in Topeka. Reid spent the entire day with Machamer who recalls the visit as 'the inspiration of his life.' When he later left the *Star* and went to New York, Machamer became associated with Reid. The association enabled Machamer to meet some of New York's leading literary and art figures and is credited by Machamer for much of his future success in the art world.

"In 1933 Albert Reid gave the University of Kansas a large collection of cartoons and magazine illustrations. Some were his own and others by such greats as Thomas Nast who crusaded against the Tweed Gang and New York's Tammany Hall. This collection is now a part of the William Allen White School of Journalism on the Lawrence campus.

"To the Albert T. Reid Collection has been added the Art Commission's highest award, the *Gold Medal of Honor.* In making the presentation the Art Commission stated: 'Albert T. Reid is the most honored and decorated of all artists.'

"Albert T. Reid was never a wealthy man. He values friendships so highly that he has scattered the fruit of his labor and talent across the nation. Hundreds of homes proudly display

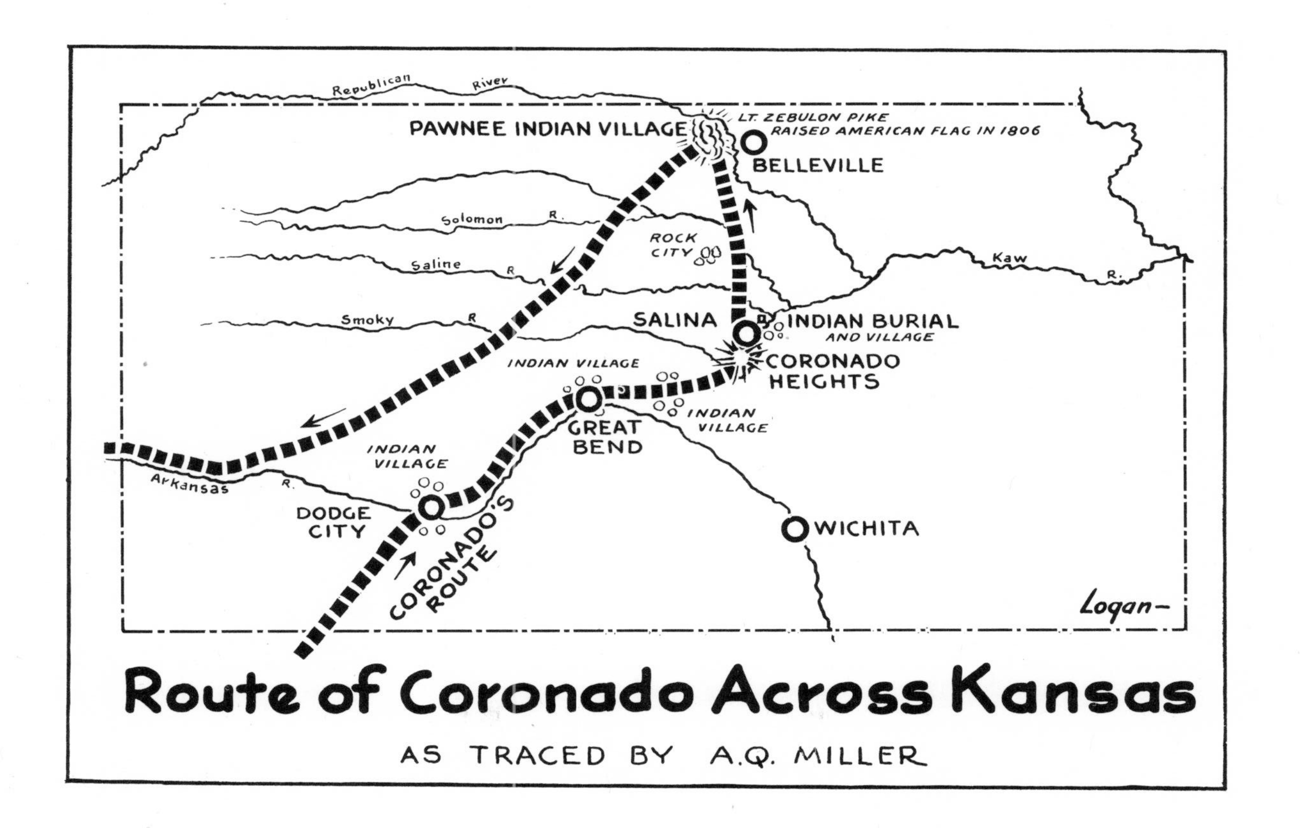

Route of Coronado Across Kansas

AS TRACED BY A.Q. MILLER

works by Albert T. Reid given as tokens of love and affection. One of my prized possessions is an autographed pen drawing of a stage coach mailed to me from New York. The drawing is entitled 'In Devil's Bend' and the locale is a couple of miles southeast of Clyde, a spot visited many times during my boyhood.

"Although a long time resident of New York, Albert Reid still retains his loyalty to Kansas."

CHAPTER XI

The Country Editor

His Responsibilities—His Rewards

EDITOR'S NOTE: *A. Q. Miller, a past president of the Kansas State Editorial Association, has served in an advisory capacity to the Kansas State School of Journalism in Manhattan, Kansas, and the William Allen White School of Journalism of the University of Kansas at Lawrence. He has frequently been called upon to address journalism classes at both of these institutions.*

The following pages, which have been prepared from Mr. Miller's lectures before journalism classes, reflect his thinking on the subject to which he has devoted his life.

IN WHAT respect does a country newspaper differ from a metropolitan newspaper? Obviously the answer is in the size of the newspaper. Wherever the circulation of a newspaper is in excess of ten thousand copies, it is generally conceded to be removed from the country newspaper category. The difference between the country and metropolitan, or city, newspaper does not lie in size alone. As a matter of fact, the country newspaper embodies an entirely different set of values and capabilities as far as the editor is concerned. It is true that the fundamentals of journalism remain the same whether one is writing a story about Farmer Brown's prize winning pig or Industrialist Jones'

Elmer T. Peterson, nationally famous journalist, a contemporary of A. Q. Miller who has referred to the publisher of the BELLEVILLE TELESCOPE *as one of Kansas and the nation's most devoted citizens.*

million dollar plant expansion. Country newspaper editing, however, requires much more than just journalistic ability. It is because the country newspaper presents such a challenge and occupies such a responsible place in the life of the community that it is one of the most satisfying and remunerative professions that one can undertake.

The remuneration is not mere money. This may sound like an old chestnut but the rewards of editing a good country newspaper are far richer than financial benefit alone. One can earn a satisfactory living as a country editor, too. With the development of new printing techniques a country newspaper plant can be purchased and operated for less investment also. The offset method of printing has enabled many journalists to launch a country newspaper where the cost of a conventional printing plant might have proven an insurmountable stumbling block.

A country newspaper editor must be more than a good journalist. He must be able to know and understand human nature as represented by his fellow townsmen; he must have a good business sense and know quite a bit about a lot of subjects. What he writes is read with interest by the people of his town as well as his rural subscribers and he had better know his subject or he'll be deluged with letters to the editor. He has to be consistently accurate in his presentation of information or the prestige of his newspaper will suffer.

While the country newspaper is actually a private business enterprise, it is something of a paradox. The general store is a private enterprise too but it can hardly be classed as a public institution. The newspaper is both a private enterprise and a public institution or servant. It must operate at a profit in order to survive and, at the same time, fulfill its role of service to the community. Yet a very rigid code of ethics govern how this newspaper can obtain its financial subsistence.

Readers rate the success of the country newspaper by its service to the community not by how much the editor is making from his venture. The measure of its success is gauged by the confidence of its readers. This confidence can only be obtained by presenting all the news honestly and openly. Presenting the news honestly, without omitting facts, distorting information, slanting the story, coloring the facts to appeal to a certain group or faction may cost the editor some financial gain but it will insure the success of his venture in the long run.

A country newspaper editor who becomes so pre-occupied with making the "fast buck" that he forgets his duty to his readers will soon lose his most precious possession: his subscribers.

The country newspaper must be independent. The editor must not allow himself to be surrounded and influenced by any pressure group. He must be a free operator, able to express his honest opinions and convictions. He must retain control of his publication and maintain its integrity at all costs.

The country newspaper is a leader in the life of the community. It does not follow the mob but rather attempts to counsel and guide the people who are its readers.

So much for the ethics of the country editor. What about the physical aspects of the country newspaper? Competition in the newspaper field is exceptionally keen. Physically the printed publication must be up to snuff or it won't be read. In many areas the large metropolitan papers circulate as much as the local paper. Readers are given a chance to compare the two and while they don't expect their local paper to have all the features and by-lined columnists that the metropolitan paper has, they do expect the typography, illustrative and writing quality of their local paper to be up to par.

The country newspaper must be kept modern in every respect and the editor must be continually on his toes. He can't afford

Z. G. Hopkins, public relations director, Western Railway Association, another Kansas journalist who shared early experiences with A. Q. Miller.

to allow his publication to become a stereotyped, lifeless production. Wherever possible he should arrange for illustrations, even though illustrations increase his production cost. His advertisements must be in good taste and have crisp clear copy as well as live art work. The advertisements in a country paper are read almost as avidly as the news pages.

Today the country newspaper presents more of a challenge than ever. The population of small towns and rural communities are as well traveled and well read as any of their big city brothers. Any attempt to write down to them will ring the death knell on the editor and his newspaper.

The country editor of today and the future will know when his newspaper is performing its service satisfactorily. A good newspaper is pointed to with pride by small town citizens. Readers will praise and respect the publication that benefits their community. For the editor, this means the satisfaction of performing a beneficial civic function. He'll find that his financial reward is adequate too and, because esthetic or moral rewards alone will not feed the editor's family, the latter is equally important.

The country newspaper very rarely has a business manager. The editor is the business manager. This presents another ethical problem. As the editor, the newspaper publisher knows what he wants to publish in his newspaper; he knows he is bound to present the news as it occurs. On the other hand in his dual role of business manager he may be approached to kill certain stories which might be detrimental to an advertiser or to use his news columns for free publicity of an advertisers commodity. Failure to cooperate with the buyer of display space may cost him money. As a business manager this is unfortunate; he knows the paper needs the money. However as the editor there can be no vacillation, the money will have to go out the window and the integrity of the paper preserved. The editor and the editor alone makes the decision and his conscience must dictate the course he is to follow.

As editor he must adopt a policy of absolute fairness and honesty in handling the news. Never will be publish gossip or scandal unless it becomes a matter of public record. When it does then it is his duty to print it, if it has news value. He must be very careful that he does not engage in personalities as far as his news pages are concerned. Human nature being what it is, the country editor isn't going to like everyone in town. He can't let these likes and dislikes in regard to individuals influence his handling of the news any more than he can permit his religious or political preference color the presentation of the news.

The same prescribed code must be followed in regard to advertisers and non-advertisers. Because a man or a business buys many pages of display advertising it does not follow that he is entitled to excessive reporting in the news columns. The man who never places a want ad is entitled to the same treatment as the largest advertiser.

The taboos listed above were true fifty years ago and they will be just as true fifty years from now. The country editor of today and the country editor of the future must abide by a rigid code of ethics. Because of his personal role in the life of the community and his almost daily contact with the readers of his newspaper his position would become untenable if he allowed himself to deviate from the proper course of action.

From time to time the death knell for the country editor and his newspaper is allegedly sounded. First it was predicted that the growth of the large metropolitan daily, which blanketed a state, would drive the small town newspaper out of existence. Then with the advent of radio the pessimists again had a field day. "Who'll want to read a newspaper when he can get all the news over his radio?" And today much the same type comment was heard when television became a reality. The *Belleville Telescope* is one of several thousand country weeklies that has withstood the so called onslaught of progress. To borrow an expression from the nation's film capital; "Country newspapers are better than ever." The progressive small town paper and its editor welcome progress, the newspaper is the harbinger of progress. Actually the greater the dissemination of news via radio and television the greater the interest in the newspaper.

If there are any embryo country editors who have been worried about the future of the country newspaper they may put their mind at ease. If anything, the well run small town paper of today and tomorrow will furnish a better livelihood than the one of the past.

The question is often asked by young journalists about whether or not the metropolitan papers offer a greater future than a career as a country journalist. The writer's experience has been limited almost exclusively to rural journalism so perhaps he isn't the best qualified person to answer that question. There is no doubt but what a career on a large metropolitan paper offers much satisfaction. It would seem that the question posed could only be answered by the individual who asked it. Certain attitudes are necessary for a successful career on a metropolitan paper and a variety of abilities are certainly required for the successful country newspaper editor. The young journalist has to make up his own mind. Fortunately he need not make his decision at once and irretrievably.

If the student of journalism has his doubts as to which field he wishes to pursue he has ample opportunity, while going to school and in the years immediately following his graduation, tc investigate both fields and find out for himself just which field seems to be the best for him. Should he decide to become a country editor, although he may not start right out as an editor, he'll find that he has embarked upon a lifetime undertaking which will reward him amply for the hard work and long hours he must put in. He'll find that he is a respected member of his community. He'll receive much gratification from the part he plays in the civic organizations of his community. He'll find ample opportunity to do a lot of good along the path of life. His family will be reared in the pleasant environment of a small town and chances are they won't be rich but they'll be comfortable. And all of a sudden the country editor will realize that he has lived almost a whole lifetime and he'll be pleased to reflect that it has been a happy and a useful one. He'll forget about the hardships and the necessary deprivations and think only of the triumphs and mostly of the hundreds of friends he has made in his community, his state and all over the nation.